Praise for *Generation Z: Born For The Storm*

Rare is the person of one generation who champions the beauty and purpose of another. Rarer still is when that message is carried by a major leader in the body of Christ. Dr. Billy Wilson is such a man, and his recent book *Generation Z: Born for the Storm* conveys both his passion and profound insight in this area. Dr. Wilson's heart for this generation is also demonstrated daily in his vision and life as he presides as president over Oral Roberts University. How refreshing it is to see a man of integrity and a strategic thinker put at the helm of a university that will truly affect the course of world history. I highly commend to you both the man and his message.

— **Bill Johnson, Bethel Church, Redding, CA,**
author of *The Way of Life* and *Born for Significance*

Dr. Billy Wilson knows the vital importance of equipping, encouraging, and empowering the generations that follow us. In *Generation Z: Born for the Storm*, Dr. Wilson combines his passion for educating young adults with his devotion for following Jesus. The result reveals the incredible impact this generation is already having on the world and shows us how we can help them fulfill the unique calling God has placed on their lives. This insightful book is a much-needed resource for this unique time in church history.

— **Pastor Chris Hodges, Senior Pastor,**
Church of the Highlands, author of *The*
Daniel Dilemma* and *Out of the Cave

Many books address issues with expertise but little experience or with experience but little expertise. However, in this book, we see that Dr. Wilson has both the academic expertise and the first-hand experience necessary to guide the church into a better understanding of how to empower Generation Z to become what just may be the greatest generation of Christians in history.

— **Pastor Stovall Weems, Senior Pastor, Celebration Church**

Dr. Billy Wilson is one of the most influential global Christian leaders. His passion and desire for the Holy Spirit and to see God move are constantly inspiring millions of people around the world. Dr. Wilson has a passion for raising up generations and unique insight and revelation that will empower and inspire whoever reads this book.

— **Pastor Russell Evans, Senior Pastor, Planetshakers Church**

John the Baptist knew who he was and what God called him to do. He was secure in his identity and clear about his destiny. He encountered God in the desert, but he also had a father who prophesied over him when he was born. God used the prophetic declaration of Zechariah to speak identity and destiny over John the Baptist. In a similar way, I believe God is releasing a prophetic declaration from fathers and mothers over this generation. In *Generation Z: Born for the Storm*, Dr. Wilson stands as a father and declares identity and mission to a generation. Along with Dr. Wilson, I am believing that we will see revival in our day because of a generation who is passionate about Jesus and willing to lay their lives down for His cause in the earth.

—Banning Liebscher,
Pastor and Founder, Jesus Culture

Generation Z: Born for the Storm is a timely invitation for the emerging generation of world changers to step into their God-appointed destiny. Dr. Wilson reminds us that the perfect storm produces the perfect setting for the natural to become supernatural. More than ever, in this pivotal time in history, Generation Z will be an essential collective of leaders who rise above to stand on God's Word and transform the world. This book will help you recognize the vast opportunities to take hold of victorious hope and your anointed purpose—and rise above any storm.

—Rob Hoskins, President, OneHope, Inc.

In a time of moral decline, social unrest, and the societal abandonment of the Word of God, Elijah's commission is still God's holy prescription: "Go anoint Elisha!" Dr. Wilson's book is an echo of that primordial call, and in this world's desperate moment, this book will be the striking of the match of another Elijah revolution. It's time to turn the hearts of the fathers to the children.

—Lou Engle, Co-founder, The Call

We are living in days where so much innovation and discovery is being made, yet so much will remain the same. The need for wisdom and experience cannot be substituted, yet at the same time, the new trends and perspectives can't be ignored.

In a very surgical manner, Dr. Billy Wilson sheds light and his leadership gems on how ministry should be done to Gen Z and how to effectively serve the church of tomorrow. This is a must-read for any leader desiring to lead effectively in the future.

— **Teofilo Hayashi, Founder, Dunamis Movement, Senior Leader, Zion Church**

Generation Z has been called to live and lead in unprecedented times. The dark clouds of surrounding storms have informed their entire earthly journey. In one small statement from this book, Dr. Wilson sets the stage to unpack the reason for and potential of this generation called Z. President Wilson has dedicated his life to reach, teach, and send Gen Z to be the answer in this world today through the power of Jesus and the Holy Spirit. *Generation Z: Born for the Storm* is a must-read!

— **Reggie Dabbs, The Youth Alliance**

In this book, Dr. Wilson highlights the distinguishing trait of Gen Z which is their readiness to embrace and adapt to change. This trait makes them survivors, equipped by God for maximum kingdom impact during a time when the world needs them the most. It is this understanding and acceptance of a generation that many find difficult to comprehend that should make us pay heed to Dr. Wilson's key insights in this book. His use of "Z" names from the Bible is illuminating and different... It will enable us to see them through the eyes of God, rather than the eyes of tradition or experience, enabling us to equip them to carry on the torch of the gospel to their own cohorts. I recommend this book as the need of the hour and trust that many will take the time and effort to read it.

—Dr. Chadwick Samuel Mohan, Lead Pastor,
New Life AG Church, Chennai, India

Generation Z: Born for the Storm is an invitation to journey alongside the unprecedented work God is doing in this generation in light of the biblical pattern found in the narrative of Scripture. Dr. Wilson speaks with an authority forged only by experience, but with the unmistakable tenderness of a pastor's heart. Whether you are leading, serving, or a part of Gen Z, this book is for you!

—Rev. Max Barroso, IPHC World Missions Ministries

This book is incredibly timely and speaks to the heart of a generation born for the storm! Dr. Wilson's heart for the next generation shines through with hope for the future of Gen Z with the inclusion of stories from the Biblical na rrative that emphasize God's ability to allow His children to soar when the winds of chaos arise. This is a must-read for any young person looking to grasp God's calling for them in this season and an inspirational message for those who are currently leading Gen Z.

—Eli Bonilla Jr., National
Millennial Director, NHCLC

Linking biblical stories of faithful men and women to the timeless truths they illustrate, Dr. Billy Wilson in *Generation Z: Born for the Storm* illustrates how today's generation of students, though raised in a world of nonstop turmoil, are perfectly equipped by God to fulfill their Kingdom destinies. *Generation Z: Born for the Storm* prophetically offers confident hope and purpose to a generation raised for such a time as this.

— **Rev. David R. Wells, M.A., D.D.,**
General Superintendent,
The Pentecostal Assemblies of Canada

Dr. William Wilson does a great service to the kingdom of God by studying its prospect on the next generation. What Dr. Wilson calls Generation Z is a young generation that is highly dynamic and full of potential. If this generation is built as a generation of faith that focuses on God, they will make a great impact on the world. To realize this vison Dr. William Wilson has made a close study of Generation Z with the mind of spiritual fatherhood. Through this book, we will be able to realize how to encourage this generation to stand as a generation with the dream of God. This is a must read for anyone interested in raising next generation servants of the Lord. I highly recommend Dr. Wilson's formidable book.

— **Younghoon Lee, PhD, Senior**
Pastor, Yoido Full Gospel Church

When I think of someone who is keen on what is in store for the upcoming generation of students, the president of a mainline university would top the list. When considering how that same generation will be positioned for ministry in the Kingdom, I place my confidence in the perspective of the leader of a Christ-centered, Spirit-filled evangelical school such as Oral Roberts University! Billy Wilson's presidency of ORU and co-chairmanship of Empowered21 has been marked with

milestones of progress within the Spirit-empowered movement. These combined leadership posts, along with his author-
ship of previous works, imminently qualifies him to bring forth
a publication that guides the anointed path of Generation Z.
But perhaps most important is Billy Wilson's proven anointing
and use of the gifts of the Spirit exemplified through decades
of dedication, preparation, and delivery of God's Word to
the masses.

— **Dr. Timothy M. Hill, Presiding Bishop,**
Church of God, Cleveland, Tennessee

As a leader in Youth With A Mission and a father of six
Generation Z children, I can wholeheartedly endorse this book
as an injection of faith and identity into what I also believe to
be one of the greatest generations in history! Generation Z is a
hero generation, willing to joyfully lay down their lives for the
cause of the Kingdom and the power of the Gospel! Dr. Billy
Wilson does an incredible job of mapping out and calling out
the remarkable DNA that God has placed in a generation that
will truly turn the world upside down! This book is for Gen Z
and about Gen Z! Everyone needs its wisdom!

–Andy Byrd, Youth With A Mission

The young men and women of Generation Z have grown
up amidst global turmoil. They are committed to cultural,
social, and political change around the world—they are our
future. As such, those of us who have come before Generation
Z have the responsibility of not only leading them well but
also learning from them. That's why I am so grateful for Dr.
Wilson's insightful and prophetic book, *Generation Z: Born for*

the Storm. Through an examination of the lives of nine biblical characters, Dr. Wilson shows us the lessons God is imparting to Gen Z believers and those they influence. No matter your age or your relationship with this dynamic generation, this book is a must-read.

—**Samuel Rodriguez, Lead Pastor, New Season Worship Center, President, National Hispanic Christian Leadership Conference, Author,** *Survive to Thrive*, **Executive Producer,** *Breakthrough* **movie**

Generation Z is a must read for those who want to lead beyond today. Max Dupree once said, "The first responsibility of leadership is to define reality." The second responsibility is to influence the future of that reality. As President of ORU and a thought leader in the highest educational and spiritual circles, no one is better qualified to define the realities of Generation Z than Dr. Billy Wilson. He is in reality a practitioner more than just a mere proclaimer. Beyond defining the realities of Generation Z, in this book, Dr. Billy Wilson has captured many insightful and helpful tools for leaders who desire to understand and influence this generation and shape the future of the church. This is a must read for older, emerging, and future leaders and influencers in the church.

—**Goodwill Shana, Senior Pastor, Word of Life Ministries (Zimbabwe), Chair of WEA International Council, Co-Chair E21 Africa Cabinet**

Generation Z: Born for the Storm is a timely word for the Church today in regard to the next generation. Generation Z is the most populous, diverse, entrepreneurial, innovative, and cause-driven generation in history. I believe this generation is one that the Church has been praying for in regard to seeing another Great Awakening take place. This is why Dr. Wilson's book is so timely as he frames for us key perspectives on how transformative Gen Z is to the world today. If you are sensing that God is setting things into motion on a global level, if you see the Holy Spirit on the move in the next generation, and if you are being prompted by the Holy Spirit to partner with the next generation, then this book is a must-read for you.

— **Terry Parkman, Empowered21 NextGen Global co-Chair, NextGen Pastor, River Valley Church**

Finally! The book about generational change we've been looking for is here. While most of the world is still obsessed with millennials, Dr. Billy Wilson understands that today, the future belongs to Generation Z. His new book *Generation Z: Born for the Storm* will change everything you know about this rising age group and the enormous influence they will have on our world. To ignore the coming impact of this generation is to do so at your peril. Get the book. It will change your outlook on the future.

— **Phil Cooke, PhD, filmmaker, media consultant, and author of *Maximize Your Influence: How to Make Digital Media Work for Your Church, Your Ministry, and You***

Generation Z has been born into the digital era; they are great communicators with a true longing for integrity and trustworthiness. They carry a mindset that gives them no problem to think outside their own box regarding building relations and act for changes they want to see. Yet they want to have true and close relations. Reading Dr. Wilson's book makes me want to put more energy into praying for and supporting the Christian leaders within Generation Z, for them to reach their own generation with the gospel. Also, since my three kids all are part of this generation, I am very thankful that this book is providing the generation itself with a strengthening challenge to give their hearts wholeheartedly as true servants of Christ.

—**Daniel Alm, General Superintendent, Swedish Pentecostal Alliance of Independent Churches**

The next generation will only be our future if we make them our present. My friend, Dr. Billy Wilson, teaches us to do just that in *Generation Z: Born for the Storm*. I encourage you to pick up a copy and take a risk on this generation. You won't regret it.

—**Nick Hall, Founder & Chief Communicator, Pulse**

Dr. Wilson is a skilled dream releaser. He has once again reminded us that Generation Z is not just the church of tomorrow, but very much the church of today. I pray this book will inspire you to release the dreams inside the Gen Zers whom you are closest to, and then, step back and watch them impact the world. They were born for such a time.

—**Doug Clay, General Superintendent, AG National Office**

God has a special plan for Generation Z! They will impact the nations for Christ. Dr. Wilson inspires and motivates you to discover the unique qualities that God is forming within this generation, as they find their potential and purpose to lead in the midst of the storm. This is a must read!

—**Daniela Freidzon, Pastor and Speaker, King of Kings Church**

Other titles by Billy Wilson

Father Cry: Healing Your Heart and the Hearts of Those You Love
Fasting Forward: Advancing Your Spiritual Life Through Fasting
As the Waters Cover the Sea: The Story of Empowered21 and the
Movement It Serves (co-authored with the late Vinson Synan)

DR. BILLY WILSON

President of ORAL ROBERTS UNIVERSITY

GENERATION

BORN FOR
THE STORM

Empowered Books
An Imprint of ORU Press
Tulsa, Oklahoma USA

Forefront
BOOKS

Generation Z: Born for the Storm

ISBN–13: 978-1-63763-027-3 (jacketed hardcover)
ISBN–13: 978-1-63763-028-0 (e-book)

Empowered Books, an imprint of ORU Press, is a regis-
tered trademark of Oral Roberts University Press.

Published by Forefront Books

Jacket & Interior Design and Composition: Hampton Creative, Tulsa, OK
Interior Design by Bill Kersey, KerseyGraphics

DEDICATION

Generation Z: Born for the Storm is dedicated to all who are a part of Generation Z. In particular, I submit this work in honor of my seven grandchildren:

Anna Wilson
Aaron Wilson
Amelia Wilson
Abi Morton
Sammy Morton
James Morton
Benjamin Morton

These living gifts to our family are a constant reminder of God's promises for new generations. Each one of them possesses amazing potential, extraordinary talent, and a bright future as part of the greatest generation in the history of the world. No matter the storms they endure, I will always be cheering them on.

I also want to express my deepest appreciation to the cadre of individuals who helped me to complete this volume. Thank you to Andrea Kabela, Kay Horner, Debbie George, Eric Peterson, Alyssa Sanders, Lisa Bowman, Dr. Mark Roberts, Dr. Charles Scott, Hampton Creative, my wife, Lisa, and a host of others who made it happen. It takes teamwork to make the dream work, and this team is the best in the world.

Additionally, special gratitude goes to the Oral Roberts University Board of Trustees for entrusting me to lead and encouraging me to write. It is a lifetime honor to serve this amazing generation of young men and women. Writing about them has truly been a delight, and daily walking alongside them has been one of my greatest pleasures.

Finally, this book is written for the students of Oral Roberts University. I am grateful for your lives and expectant for what God will do through you both now and in the years to come. Always remember: you were *born for the storm*.

CONTENTS

LIST OF ILLUSTRATIONS

INTRODUCTION
A PERFECT STORM

Positive! This usually encouraging word sent fear through the earth as millions of people's tests confirmed that they had contracted coronavirus or COVID-19 during the once-in-a-century pandemic of 2020–2021. The day the word "positive" appeared on an official medical email to my wife, Lisa, announcing her antigen test result, it sent shock waves through our family. Within moments, we were taking steps to isolate Lisa and move me to another area where I would quarantine for ten days. Lisa's asthma caused us additional concern as we faced her bout with the killer virus. Thankfully, after a few days of sickness, she rebounded quickly, tested negative, and survived an ordeal that has officially claimed more than a million lives globally. During my ten days in quarantine, I tested negative two different times and successfully survived my extreme staycation intact. Never has the word *negative* been so positive.

The pandemic shook the world and challenged all of us as never before. Schools closed, classes moved online, and life passages—like graduations, weddings, and even funerals—were postponed or canceled. Travel was halted, restaurants shifted to carryout, sporting events were scratched, masks were donned, and we were told to distance ourselves from others. This was all in the interest of slowing the spread of the virus and reducing the number of positive cases.

In many ways, the pandemic was part of a twenty-first-century perfect storm swirling in the world. The movie *The Perfect Storm*, starring George Clooney, depicts the story found in a nonfiction book of the same name, written by Sebastian Junger.[1] Junger relates the dramatic account of a commercial fishing vessel called *Andrea Gail* and her captain Billy Tyne, played by Clooney in the movie. *Andrea Gail* attempted to sail—without success—through a 1991 "perfect storm" that included a tropical depression-turned-hurricane off the coast of Newfoundland. A rogue wave crashed into the ship, causing it to sink with no survivors. Despite the efforts of a courageous crew, the storm was simply too big and too powerful to overcome.

In many ways, what feels like a perfect storm surrounds this generation in the twenty-first century. The relatively calm waves, interrupted by periodic turbulence, that were experienced by previous generations have given way to a tumultuous life-sea where the waves are high, the winds are strong, the intensity is unceasing, and the challenges feel insurmountable. This book is about the generation at the center of this increasing storm—Generation Z.

While the *Andrea Gail* was unable to sail through the storm, despite the courage and determination of her crew, Gen Z has the potential to not only *survive* the perfect storm of this day but also to *thrive* in the midst of it. This new generation, born between 1997 and 2012,[2] has never witnessed a calm sea. Social harmony, economic stability, physical tranquility, and domestic peace have all been very distant during this period. While those of us from earlier generations are often disturbed by it all, Generation Z considers these storms a part of their existence. They are survivors, and they are being equipped by God for maximum kingdom impact during a time when the world needs them the most.

Generation Z: Born for the Storm is written as a book of hope for this new generation. We will examine the environment surrounding Gen Z and try to understand who they are. We will also look at the unique qualities God is forming in Gen Z believers. I have attempted to be both inspirationally descriptive in identifying qualities already emerging and also prophetically aspirational in predicting qualities that will emerge as Gen Zers take their place of leadership in the world. Every chapter focuses on a person or persons from the Bible whose names begin with "Z" and who embody qualities God is forming in this new generation. This is not an exhaustive volume that details everything about Gen Z. It is simply a snapshot in time connected to the timeless truths of Scripture that will allow us to reflect upon, respond to, and empower what I believe is the most important generation to ever live. I am honored and grateful that God has given me an opportunity to love and serve them. Their potential is beyond description.

The rogue waves of the perfect storm surrounding us will sink those vessels attempting to sail by their own strength. The pressure of these waves of turmoil will be crushing. Many will shipwreck and not survive. Yet for those who follow Christ fully, the giant waves of this perfect storm will propel us forward like the waves of the ocean thrust forth a surfer.

I have always been amazed at those who challenge the largest waves on earth. From Hawaii and California to Australia and Portugal, these giant wave surfers rise to conquer what would kill others. Riding waves that reach heights of more than fifty feet, they position themselves in a way that the energy of the wave propels them forward rather than taking them under. The result is terrifying exhilaration and amazing speeds of up to fifty miles an hour. Spirit-empowered believers in Generation Z are now being positioned in a way that the giant breakers of spiritual turbulence in our generation will serve as a propellant, pushing them beyond any generation before. Yes, the terrifying exhilaration will also be used by God as a supernatural accelerant. The storm will carry them to the ends of the earth with the message of Jesus Christ.

Just as with the COVID-19 tests, when every "negative" was a "positive," Gen Z will take the negative circumstances they have been given and, by God's grace, turn them into positives. Generation Z is ready. God is equipping. The Holy Spirit is moving. The world is waiting. The winds are blowing, and the waves are roaring. Spiritual history is going to be made because Generation Z is *born for the storm*!

CHAPTER ONE

A GENERATION BORN TO LEAD: "ZEKE"

Generation Z has been called to live and lead in unprecedented times. The dark clouds of surrounding storms have informed their entire earthly journey. Rarely in history has any one generation endured so many history-making, tumultuous events in so few years as today's teenagers and youth have experienced. Physical, sociological, emotional, and spiritual storms have been a way of life for them. Those born between 1995 and 2012[3] have lived in a world filled with disarray and consistent prophetic energy. Many of today's young people have already experienced more personal and corporate disorder than my generation, the "baby boomer" generation, has experienced throughout our entire lifetime. And Gen Z is just getting started.

For one, they have endured the ongoing storm of terrorism and shootings in America. The events of September 11, 2001, ushered in a new age of violence and radicalism throughout the world, evidenced by the collapse of the Twin Towers of the World Trade Center in New York City. Generation Z was marked by this event. I can relate to this some; I still remember where I was standing as a five-year-old on November 22, 1963, when President John F. Kennedy was assassinated. I remember watching the black-and-white television in horror as the news anchor described the president being shot and fatally wounded while riding in a Lincoln convertible in a ten-mile motorcade through the streets of downtown Dallas. Thirty minutes later, the thirty-fifth president of the United States was pronounced dead at only forty-six years of age.[4] My entire generation was marked by the violence and upheaval of that day. I also remember where I was on 9/11, and I recall the sense of terror unleashed across America, but Gen Z's childhood was shaped by this event and by events of the years that followed. Children watched as terrorism not only permeated the world but also struck fear into their communities, schools, and families.

Between 2007 and 2017, an average of 21,000 deaths per year were due to terrorism. In 2014, global deaths as a result of terrorism hit an all-time high of 44,490, constituting roughly 0.05 percent of all deaths around the world.[5] Terrorism has not only been a global phenomenon; it has also become a local reality on an entirely new scale with the rise of mass shootings and random violence.

A 2018 American Psychological Association study called *Stress in America* stated that 75 percent of Gen Zers reported mass shootings as a significant source of stress for them.[6] It is no wonder since on average, at least four people have been killed in a mass shooting every forty-seven days since June 17, 2015.[7] According to *The Washington Post*, there have been school shootings in forty-three of the fifty states, occurring at a rate of about once per month, since the year 2000.[8]

Another storm Gen Zers have endlessly endured is the storm of natural disasters, which seems to have escalated in frequency and impact throughout their lifetime. Hurricanes, tsunamis, tornadoes, earthquakes, floods, wildfires, and droughts have all been part of this generation's life experience. Smartphones and social media have brought these natural storms close, allowing us to receive eyewitness reports on the destruction and tragedy. Over the last 15 years, global natural disasters have cost trillions of dollars in damage and affected billions of people. The year 2017 was the US's costliest on record, with sixteen different disasters resulting in at least $1 billion in damage each.

Overall, the US lost $300 billion from natural disasters in that one year alone.[9]

There has also been a persistent storm of health crises in the world throughout Gen Z's lifetime. In November 2002, SARS (Severe Acute Respiratory Syndrome) was first identified in China. By July 2003, more than 8,000 cases and 774 deaths occurred. In 2009, H1N1 swine flu sickened 575,000, resulting in 18,500 deaths. In 2012, about 122,000 people died of measles, and tuberculosis killed an estimated 1.3 million people. Beginning in 2014 and over the course of two years, the Ebola virus killed more than 11,300 people in West Africa and threatened to become a global pandemic. In 2015–16, there were 5,186 Zika virus cases in the US and many more throughout the world. In 2019, we experienced the highest number of measles cases since 1992.[10] And in 2020 and 2021, we face the worldwide impact of the coronavirus, or COVID-19, resulting in more than 166 million cases and deaths exceeding 3.4 million at the time of this writing.[11] Unlike any other health crisis in modern history, the COVID-19 contagion swept the world in record time with horrific results. Nations shut down their economies and borders as people sheltered in place. Generation Z students were sent home from school to learn at a distance. Public events were canceled, churches dismissed their services, and the travel industry screeched to a halt. Fear swept the globe as the cruel coronavirus wreaked havoc worldwide.

Still, the aforementioned storms are just the tip of the iceberg. Many other whirlwinds of uncertainty have spun around today's youth during the last two decades, including economic downturns and recessions, racial division and riots, domestic and sexual abuse, identity confusion, and a plethora of other adversarial winds. When we reflect on what has happened in our world during the first two decades of the twenty-first century, we understand more clearly the unrelenting pressure Gen Z finds itself under. It is little wonder that mental crises are at an all-time high. The more we read these statistics, research history, and study Scripture, the clearer it becomes that our culture is on a collision course — not with a meteor, but with a Master! We are in the days that Jesus foretold would precede His second coming.

God is not surprised by the chaos of our time, so we should not be either. Jesus prophesied, "There will be great earthquakes, famines and pestilences in various places, and fearful events and great signs from heaven."[12] He further predicted, "There will be signs in the sun, moon and stars. On the earth, nations will be in anguish and perplexity at the roaring and tossing of the sea. People will faint from terror, apprehensive of what is coming on the world, for the heavenly bodies will be shaken."[13] The gospel writer Matthew records Christ's description of how nations will engage in war with each other, natural disasters will plague the earth, and Christians will be intensely persecuted.[14] He

This new generation was born for this day. Gen Z will not only survive the storms but will thrive in the midst of them. In fact, the storms will help shape them into leaders during these greatest days in the history of the world.

foretells that "this gospel of the kingdom will be preached in the whole world as a testimony to all nations, and then the end will come."[15]

These passages make this truth clear: We are in the final days. Or as we could call it — *the final storm*. Though we do not know how long this tempest will persist, I do believe that God has called Gen Z to fulfill their destiny in these tumultuous times. This new generation was born for this day. Gen Z will not only survive the storms but will thrive in the midst of them. In fact, the storms will help shape them into leaders during these greatest days in the history of the world.

Time to Soar

Birds move through the air in various ways. Some fly by flapping — like hummingbirds, whose incessant energy keeps them suspended. Others fly by gliding — like songbirds leaving a limb to land near food and moving from one place to another without flapping their wings. Gliding allows a bird to ride the wind, but it *always* leads downward, just like an airplane glider, which rides the wind's currents but ultimately lands on the ground.

Eagles are different, though. They belong to a select group of birds that have the capacity to *soar*. While gliding always leads downward, even if slowly or intermittently, soaring allows a bird to climb upward without ever flapping its wings. Eagles rely on thermal updrafts to carry them to amazing heights. Even and *especially* around storms, where updrafts are pronounced, an eagle can use the thermal currents of the storm to rise higher — *if* he is willing to face into the wind.

I believe this generation will do exactly that. They will face the turmoil of the storm with confidence, using the updrafts of its turbulence to rise higher and go farther than ever before. They will not run away from the pressure. They will not quit; they will *soar*! Isaiah declared, "Even youths grow tired and weary, and young men stumble and fall; but those who hope in the LORD will renew their strength. They will soar on wings like eagles; they will run and not grow weary, they will walk and not be faint."[16]

One person who used the stormy winds surrounding him in his generation to soar high as a leader was Winston Churchill. Churchill had a storied political career before World War II, but it was during this "storm of a century" that he emerged as a global leader and one of the great heroic figures of the last hundred years. Churchill led the United Kingdom in the midst of horrific chaos throughout World War II. During this era, Hitler was running free across Europe and attacking Britain incessantly. Other Axis powers were threatening Britain's allies and interests all around the world. The Japanese had captured Singapore in 1942, two years before D-Day. During this difficult time, Churchill uttered these famous words: "The whole future of mankind may depend upon our conduct. So far, we have not failed. We shall not fail now. Let us move forward steadfastly together into the storm and through the storm."[17]

Churchill discerned the storm of his day. It was severe, yet he believed that the United Kingdom and its allies could navigate through it. The turbulent winds of his time pushed Churchill higher as a leader and provided a context that would reveal his leadership prowess. The powerful thermals and dynamics of the World War II storm elevated Churchill immensely. I believe the same will happen with this new generation as they face the storms that surround them.

As with Churchill, a new wave of leaders will emerge in stormy times like these. They will be leaders who are ready to embrace the challenges pervading their age. These Gen Z leaders will not run from the trials of their generation but will courageously face them, understanding that it is their destiny to lead through the storm. They will use the tempestuous winds they encounter to soar high. These types of leaders are found throughout history and Scripture. They are described in Proverbs 28:2 in this way: "When the country is in chaos, everybody has a plan to fix it—But it takes a leader of real understanding to straighten things out" (MSG). I believe Gen Z is filled with leaders like this— leaders who are *born for the storm.*

Scripture gives us a perfect example of two leaders who responded very differently to their storms. One Old Testament narrative reveals a leader who was born for the storm. In the New Testament church, we are shown a model for using the storm to soar.

"ZEKE"

Our first leader is the Old Testament prophet Ezekiel, but we will refer to him as "Zeke." His name means "God strengthens,"[18] and this name proved to be key to his leadership. Zeke was born into a storm. The nation of Judah had drifted from God, and the resulting storm of judgment surrounded Zeke during his early life. Political upheaval, military defeat, economic collapse, and societal disorder all culminated in Ezekiel's displacement to a foreign land. The spiritual reformation attempted by King Josiah failed, and scarcely more than a decade after the death of Josiah, Judah surrendered to the armies of the north. Young Ezekiel was among the first prisoners deported to Babylonia in 597 BC. In Babylon, Zeke was placed in a camp of God's people located at Tel Abib on the Kebar (Chebar) canal (near Nippur).[19] This canal encampment was in Babylon, in what is now the country of Iraq.

The book of Ezekiel begins with this young priest living in an Iraqi (Babylonian) prison camp, far from home, enduring the ravages of war, terribly battered by the multiyear turmoil of being an exiled prisoner in a foreign land. Zeke's life was filled with storms, so it is probably not surprising that God appeared to him in the midst of one. Many times, we see God's greatest glory in the midst of our storms. The disciples were in a storm when Jesus came to them walking on the water. Job was faced with the greatest storm of his life when he saw God's glory and was restored.

The same was true for Ezekiel. He begins his autobiography in prophecy, stating that while he was living with the exiles by the Kebar River, the heavens opened, and he saw visions of God. His first vision started with a storm. "I looked, and I saw a windstorm coming out of the north—an immense cloud with flashing lightning and surrounded by brilliant light,"[20] he wrote. The prophet's incredible encounter with God and ultimate calling began in what seemed to be a *thunderstorm*. The glory of God would soon be unveiled to Ezekiel from the middle of this storm, permeated with amazing visions. God's appearance left him so stunned that he fell on his face. By the end of Zeke's first chapter, we find the young prophet lying prostrate on Babylonian soil, overwhelmed by the storm of God's presence and the circumstances of captivity. Empty, humbled, disoriented, and weakened, he was ready to hear God's voice.

As He addressed the humbled refugee, God instructed Ezekiel to shift his posture and simultaneously empowered him with His Spirit to raise him to his feet: "He said to me, 'Son of man, stand up on your feet and I will speak to you.' As he spoke, the Spirit came into me and raised me to my feet, and I heard him speaking to me."[21]

He discovered what our generation must discover: God can be found in the midst of the storm! God's purpose for Ezekiel's life flowed out of the storm he was living in and from the storm of God's presence he witnessed.

At this moment, young Zeke was lifted to his feet and commissioned to prophesy to his generation. He was called to minister both to exiles and to those still in Jerusalem, predicting further judgment while also bringing future hope. Ezekiel was raised up as a leader in the midst of the storm of his generation. He discovered what our generation must discover: God can be found in the midst of the storm! God's purpose for Ezekiel's life flowed out of the storm he was living in and from the storm of God's presence he witnessed.

The turbulent events that landed Zeke in Babylon were used by God to position him for a visitation. The pain of his imprisonment opened the door for his destiny. We would have never heard of Ezekiel without the storms he encountered.

Generation Z must understand that although God has not caused all the storms they have encountered, He *can* be found in the midst of them. The storm of Ezekiel's day did not end with God's thunderous revelation by the river, but God gave young Zeke the strength and power necessary to stand up during the storms ahead. Ezekiel was *born for the storm,* and God used him as an instrument of hope for his generation. After all, his name means "God strengthens"! So, when the storm leaves the Gen Zers in our lives on their faces and they feel their strength is gone, we must remind them of Zeke. We must encourage them to listen for God's voice and allow the wind of His presence to direct them toward their destiny of leadership.

Leadership in the Storm: Paul

Like Gen Zers, the apostle Paul was also born into a generational storm (in addition to facing a *real*, physical storm we will discuss later). Because he embraced God's plan in the midst of these storms, he emerged as an incredibly influential leader in his day. The last few chapters of the book of Acts record that Paul was arrested in Jerusalem and incarcerated in the port city of Caesarea, where he remained in prison for two years. Paul appealed to Caesar for trial, and he was put on a ship in Caesarea and sent toward Rome. Upon arrival, he planned to defend both himself and Christianity in Caesar's court.

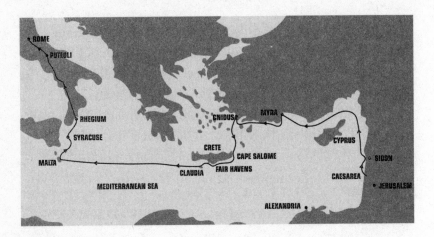

FIG. 1.1: Map showing route of Paul's journey to Rome[22]

Paul's prison vessel started from Caesarea and traveled north along the eastern coast of the Mediterranean to avoid contrary winds. The prison ship circled Cypress, sailed over to Myra, and continued toward Crete, and a decision was made to continue sailing despite the approaching winter. This journey may not seem incredibly long on paper, but to the 250-plus passengers who endured storms, violent seas, a shipwreck, and months stranded on Malta, it not only seemed like years, but it actually took a year or more.

On Paul's voyage from Caesarea, he was not known as a great apostle or missionary. He was simply a prisoner in chains. No one looked to him for leadership. No one asked for his advice. Still, even without man's initial recognition, he emerged as a leader in a major storm—both a metaphorical and physical storm. This is the path many Gen Z leaders will follow. They will emerge from the unknown, nameless galleys of our day to lead in the midst of the storm. As we follow Paul in his journey, several leadership lessons emerge for those of us who are born for the storm.

PERCEPTION AND INSIGHT

Paul's voyage across the Mediterranean began in October, which means the captain planned to sail through the winter. From the start, this was destined to be a dangerous feat. As the ship prepared to leave the safe haven in Crete, Paul communicated an important insight to his fellow passengers. Before they set sail toward Rome, he said, "Men, I can see that our voyage is going to be disastrous and bring great loss to ship and cargo, and to our own lives also."[23] It did not take a genius to understand the dangers of sailing in the winter, but Paul was imparting spiritual insight beyond the norm. He was speaking with clear foresight about something much bigger and more disastrous than cold weather. That is what leaders do. They face their present reality head-on while anticipating the future they will enter into.

You, like Paul, were born with insight. If you are filled with the Holy Spirit, you too have been given perception beyond the natural. A 2007 article in the *New York Times* said this about leadership and disaster: "In times of consuming trauma, psychologists and historians say, a leader must speak with a trusted voice and sketch honestly the painful steps to safety. A leader must weave a narrative of shared loss while acknowledging consuming anger."[24] This is what Paul did throughout this harrowing expedition.

Just as Paul predicted, as soon as the ship left the harbor, adversity ensued. The mild, warm breeze, once helping them sail comfortably, transformed into a feared northeaster. The cold winds and rains came sweeping across the Mediterranean in sheets of terror. They knew a storm like this could easily destroy any ship daring to sail into it. The winds blew with a chilling gale force. They put ropes under the bottom of the vessel to hold it together, and they took down the mainsail so that it would not break in the wind. Their situation seemed hopeless as the winds blew them toward shipwreck. The rain pelted the passengers for fourteen days, setting them adrift on a two-week, terror-filled voyage. When the wind and rain finally subsided, the passengers realized where they were—in the middle of nowhere. Upon this realization, Paul demonstrated the second set of qualities necessary to lead in the midst of the storm.

COURAGE AND CONFIDENCE

At this juncture on their journey, Paul exhibited great bravery and poise when he addressed his fellow passengers, who were so terrified. He said, "'But now I urge you to keep up your courage, because not one of you will be lost; only the ship will be destroyed. Last night an angel of the God to whom I belong and whom I serve stood beside me and said, 'Do not be afraid, Paul. You must stand trial before Caesar; and God has graciously given you the lives of all who sail with you.'"[25]

When the wind threatens to blow us off course, we can tune into heaven, receive a word from God, and continue to lead through the storm.

Paul's confidence in the midst of chaos came not because he was without fear but because he had a word from God. God's Word infused him with courage and confidence. The fact is that in the midst of the storm, chaos can easily rob us of confidence. Yet, when the wind threatens to blow us off course, we can tune into heaven, receive a word from God, and continue to lead through the storm.

This key leadership quality is why, at Oral Roberts University, we intentionally prioritize hearing God's voice. We ask students regularly, "Have you heard God's voice? Do you have a word from Him?" When you have a word from God, what the winds are doing does not matter. How high or how rough the waves may be is irrelevant. Why? Because you know God is going to get you through the storm. In fact, you know it so well that you can confidently encourage others with His truth, as you encourage yourself. That is what Paul did. Essentially, he said, "Don't worry, men. The ship is going under, but you're staying up. God is going to save our lives! I have a word from Him that we are going to be all right—even in the midst of the storm."

CLARITY AND DECISIVENESS

After two weeks of enduring the terrible storm and being blown completely off course, Paul and the crew found themselves nearing land. They threw down four anchors from the stern, which held the ship in the rear. Fear overtook some crew members who felt their vessel was headed for shipwreck. They planned to use lifeboats, sail to shore, save their own lives, and leave the prisoners to die. At that moment, Paul discerned that he must immediately speak up. He confidently said to the captain, "Unless these men stay with the ship, you cannot be saved."[26]

Can you imagine how Paul felt uttering these words? There he was, having endured two weeks of violent weather, having held on to insight and a word from God when all hope seemed lost, and now he was hearing that the crew wanted to leave him and the other prisoners to die. In a moment, he had to act with Holy Spirit-inspired decisiveness and clarity. So, he stepped to the bow of the ship and addressed them. And because he did, the captain stopped the sailors from leaving. This was the defining moment in which a leader emerged in the midst of a storm. Because Paul had insight, courage, and authority—stepping forward with a voice demanding respect—those who were supposed to be his authority listened to and obeyed *him*.

Chaos always demands clarity. It demands that you make decisions both quickly and accurately as you are intentionally led by the Holy Spirit. As Christian author John Maxwell says, "A leader is one who knows the way, goes the way, and shows the way."[27]

FOCUSED PEACE

At last, with the boat anchored, Paul, along with the other passengers, anxiously awaited daylight. Here, his next leadership quality was revealed: the quality of focused peace. At this point, it was still storming, and passengers were still fearing their fate. In spite of this, Paul knew what was ahead, so he said to them, "Now I urge you to take some food. You need it to survive. Not one of you will lose a single hair from his head."[28] Then, he prayed over his bread, broke it, and ate.

Let's picture this for a moment. The winds were still blowing. The rain had not stopped. And there was Paul—having lunch. Remind you of someone? Throughout the gospels, we see Jesus reflect a similar, focused peace. He was never intimidated by the storm. He was never worried about it. In fact, at one point, he was asleep in the bottom of a boat in the midst of a horrifying squall!

Many years ago, English minister John Wesley encountered a group of Christians who exhibited this same trait. He was returning to the New World from England,[29] where he had been ministering, though it is clear from his writings that he felt the mission was unsuccessful. On his journey home, a great storm arose in the Atlantic. The ship he was on was tossed harshly up and down. The storm became so intense that Wesley ventured from his cabin to the top of the ship to see what was going on. He observed the waves crashing as the winds nearly knocked him from his feet. Initially, he was terrified. But then, he noticed something in stark contrast to his setting. He watched and listened in awe as a group of Moravian Christians sang hymns unto God on the deck of the boat. They were having a worship service in the middle of the storm!

Wesley was inspired by their assurance of faith — something he was struggling with. He envied the trust in Christ that they had and the peace that came with it. Upon returning to England, Wesley sought out the Moravians, wanting to discover the secret to their peace. It was not until he "went very unwillingly to a society at Aldersgate Street" that his heart became "strangely warmed." He found the peace he had sought, and both his life and ministry were changed forever.[30] Wesley eventually became known as a key figure in the First Great Awakening in America and the Evangelical Revival in England. What changed things that caused the gospel to come alive to him? The Moravians who, in the midst of the storm — perhaps even as they were about to lose their lives — exuded focused peace, fully trusting that God was in control. Isaiah encouraged Judah and any nation that keeps faith, "You will keep in perfect peace those whose minds are steadfast, because they trust in you. Trust in the LORD forever, for the LORD, the LORD himself, is the Rock eternal."[31]

RESILIENCE

During the ship's final push toward the shore of Malta, it ran aground on a sandbar, and waves pummeled the small craft to pieces. Every sailor and prisoner aboard, all longing to step foot on land again, either swam the rest of the way to the shore or grabbed a piece of wood and floated there. Just as Paul had prophesied, no one lost their life. The passengers and sailors stood on the shore *alive*. They were dripping wet and freezing cold but still very much alive.

On days when the enemy attacks, the serpent bites at the worst time, and you feel you have been pushed beyond the brink, you can adopt this leadership quality of resilience.

As they stood shivering onshore, the northeastern winds cut through them like an arctic blast, so they gathered wood to build a fire. Paul tossed a branch onto the growing flame, and a snake that had been hibernating in the timber leaped from it and attached itself to his hand. Those around him saw the snake bite Paul, so they began saying of their visitor, "This man must be a murderer; for though he escaped from the sea, the goddess Justice has not allowed him to live. But Paul shook the snake off into the fire and suffered no ill effects."[32] What a testimony! In times when nothing seems to be going right—when your ship does not come in, your path takes a major detour, or you feel cold, abandoned, and forsaken—you can follow Paul's example. On days when the enemy attacks, the serpent bites at the worst time, and you feel you have been pushed beyond the brink, you can adopt this leadership quality of resilience.

Resilience is the capacity to recover quickly from difficulties. It is toughness. Imagine how Paul felt. He had just endured so much—a horrific storm, attempted betrayal, harsh weather conditions with no shelter—and now this! A snakebite! But did he sulk or pout or give up? No—he shook it off. He persevered, and he suffered no ill effects. As it was with Paul, there will be seasons in our lives when we will seem to encounter trouble over and over again. When it feels like the storm will not stop, we can take heart. God will preserve us. True leaders are the ones who *always* get back up and demonstrate resilience.

POWER

As it became obvious to the people sitting around the fire that Paul had not been harmed by the snakebite, word spread. They felt they had come into contact with someone touched by God. People began asking him to pray for their sick loved ones, and doors opened for him to spread the gospel. One account was when one of the island leaders' "father was sick in bed, suffering from fever and dysentery. Paul went in to see him and, after prayer, placed his hands on him, and God healed him. When this had happened, the rest of the sick on the island came and were cured."[33]

There Paul was—in a barbaric place—unable to speak the people's language, yet he kept moving up in leadership while on the island of Malta. It will be the same for you. When God's hand is on you, He will keep elevating you to strategic leadership levels despite any attacks or negative circumstances.

FROM STORM TO PLATFORM

Another narrative in Scripture exhibits this type of power. It occurred just after Jesus fed five thousand people who had come to hear Him teach. He instructed the disciples to go in a boat across the Sea of Galilee as He went up to a mountain to pray. While they were out at sea, a storm came, and they were terrified. Jesus came down from the mountain and walked through the storm on the top of the sea. When He neared the disciples' boat, they noticed Him, and thinking He was a ghost, they grew even more afraid.[34] But Jesus said to them, "Take courage! It is I. Don't be afraid." Then Peter, one of the disciples, responded, "Lord, if it's you...tell me to come to you on the water."[35] Jesus beckoned, and Peter walked on water.

Jesus was completely undeterred, unfettered, and unbroken by the storm that surrounded Him. Peter was too, as long as he kept his eyes on Jesus. The waves continued to beat, the rain continued to fall, and the wind continued to hurl across the lake, but none of that had power over Him. He walked above it, and so did Peter. The storm became their platform!

Like Zeke, we can see God's glory in the midst of the storm and find the strength to stand up in our destiny. Like Paul, we can demonstrate perception and insight, speak with courage and confidence, and act with decisiveness and clarity. We can demonstrate supernatural peace, resilience, and power while others fret and collapse under pressure. We can emerge in the midst of the storm as the leaders God has called us to be. And, like the apostle Peter, we can turn our storm into our platform as we focus on Jesus and obey His word. Yes, Generation Z has been born into one of the greatest days of turmoil and upheaval the world has ever known. Yet, God is calling them to rise above the chaos and to lead in the midst of the storm.

CHAPTER TWO
A GENERATION BORN FOR A PURPOSE: ZAPHENATH-PANEAH

Defining any generation is not easy, but this is especially true of a generation that seems to be characterized by individualism, resisting group labels at every turn.

Most sociologists define Generation Z as those individuals born approximately between 1997 and 2012. They carry notable differences from the previous generation known as "millennials." Numerous words are used to describe this group of young people, including "communicators," "justice-driven," "technology natives," "pragmatic," "innovators," "entrepreneurs," and "single-minded world-changers." This is a peculiar group of people who seem more determined than ever to achieve and enjoy a purpose-filled life, and I am certain they will do an extraordinary work on earth. Gen Z represents the future of our country and the potential of our world. They are the group of people I spend nearly three-quarters of my week with and the army of young people I believe can and *will* make a lasting mark on the earth for Christ.

As the president of a university, I have the unique opportunity to regularly rub shoulders with Gen Z students. I spend a significant amount of time with them in meetings, events, classes, informal discussions, and even sleeping a few nights each year in the men's dorms during my annual "Resident President" week. Yet, I am always learning new things about them. In fact, being around this generation pushes me to know all I can. They are a fascinating group of people, and I love what I continually discover about them. Every bit of information—whether learned by experience or through reading others' insights—sheds new, refreshing light on who exactly this *now* generation is and how they just might change our world forever. One such insight comes from *The Gen Z Effect* by Thomas M. Koulopoulos and Dan Keldsen. The table presented in their book conveys shifts in perspectives Gen Z has already begun to initiate.

PERSPECTIVE ON:	BEFORE GEN Z:	AFTER GEN Z:
Internet access	A privilege	A human right
Influence	Purchased	Earned
Failure	Avoided	Embraced
Uncertainty	Prepared for	Predicted
Retirement	A destination	A journey
Connectivity	A luxury	A necessity

Table 2.1: Perspectives of Generation Z[36]

Unquestionably, this list indicates that one of the driving forces behind Gen Z's choices can be summarized by one word that I have inserted at the bottom of the list—*purpose*. Zach Mercurio wrote in an article for *HuffPost*, "The newest generation to enter the workforce, Generation Z, should be called 'The Purpose Generation.'"[37] What he discovered, and many others are discovering, is that purpose is a *big deal* to this generation, and its emphasis bleeds into every facet of their lives. As stated by Mercurio, it would benefit someone who seeks to

Purpose is a *big deal* to this generation, and its emphasis bleeds into every facet of their lives.

hire from this generation to know Gen Z is searching to "discover a purpose that is worth committing to—one that is socially responsible, human-centered, and ethical."[38]

According to Sparks and Honey, a marketing research company that compiles data and reports on culture, Gen Z exhibits the following traits regarding work-life:

- They are eager to start working.
- They are mature and in control.
- They learned that traditional choices do not guarantee success.
- They communicate with symbols, speed, and images.
- Their social circles are global.
- Entrepreneurship is in their DNA. (72 percent of high school students want to start a business someday.)
- They intend to change the world.[39]

If like me, you were born before Generation Z, remember this: we would be unwise to unknowingly and insensitively group millennials and Gen Zers together or confuse the two. Generation Z has *real* differences, strengths, and weaknesses that are worth paying attention to.

Recently, I shared a series of chapel messages with our students about their generation. A lot of things surprised me when researching for this, but the most surprising piece of information honestly came from some of their responses. Many of them actually thought they were millennials! It was not until I began describing research-based characteristics of Gen

Z that they started identifying with their generation and recognizing their unique qualities. This highlights an important point. If like me, you were born before Generation Z, remember this: we would be unwise to unknowingly and insensitively group millennials and Gen Zers together or confuse the two. Generation Z has *real* differences, strengths, and weaknesses that are worth paying attention to.

The Lovell Corporation confirmed this in their recent report, titled "The Change Generation Report," in which they stated that the top five work value priorities have changed drastically between the two generations as table 2 illustrates.

MILLENNIALS	GENERATION Z
Job security	Interesting work
Interesting work	Organization you're proud of
Convenient hours of work	Work you're passionate about
Work-life balance	Having the information to do your job
Continuous learning	Continuous learning

Table 2.2: Five work priority comparisons between millennials and Generation Z[40]

We see the effects of these changes clearly throughout our university's student body. A few years ago, our leadership teams began noticing that the student composition was shifting and the things we *thought* we knew about the students were simply not working. This pushed us to research, study, and reach a new understanding of the students coming to our campus. These changes among our students served as a major inspiration for me to write this book. Generation Z is different from millennials in many ways, but one difference I see often is in their motivations and drive. Gen Z is driven to make a positive difference. They seem to carry a generational gifting around purpose.

Competitive Solutions, Inc., a Georgia-based business management consulting company, says this about the *now* generation: "Generation Z wants more than just a job; they seek a job with purpose, a sense of fulfillment that helps to move the world forward."[41] Shane Pruitt, pastor, speaker, and author, stated in a *Church Leaders* magazine article titled "Ten Characteristics of Gen Z" that "Generation Z is globally minded and wants their life to matter. They are fully aware of their imperfections, evil, hate, and injustices. They are looking for solutions, answers, and impact. They're not scared to die young; however, they are terrified to die at a ripe old age and have done nothing significant with their lives in their own age."[42]

This is a generation driven by purpose. Still, even with immense passion, Generation Z, like every generation before them, will be ill-equipped to discover and fulfill their God-given purpose without previous generations well-prepared to guide them. As you read through the chapters of this book, I hope you are both inspired and informed about how *you* can help the Gen Zers in your life become all they are destined to be. And if you are a Gen Zer, I hope that you are more motivated and challenged than ever before to pursue the God-given purpose burning on the inside of you. The New Testament writer Luke quoted Paul's sermon, "Now when David had served God's purposes in his generation, he fell asleep."[43] I sincerely believe that just as David served God's purposes in his generation, every Gen Zer can serve God's purposes in this generation. Let's talk about how.

ZAPHENATH-PANEAH

Our "Z" person for this chapter is Zaphenath-Paneah. That name is a mouthful and not the familiar name we typically use for this biblical character. We know him as Joseph; however, "Pharaoh gave Joseph the name Zaphenath-Paneah and gave him Asenath daughter of Potiphera, priest of On, to be his wife. And Joseph went throughout the land of Egypt. Joseph was thirty years old when he entered the service of Pharaoh king of Egypt. And Joseph went out from Pharaoh's presence and traveled throughout Egypt."[44]

Zaphenath-Paneah. This Egyptian name means "the one who furnishes the nourishment of life,"[45] or "revealer of secrets."[46] Joseph was well-known throughout his nation—the most powerful nation in the world in his time. God's purpose for Joseph included becoming a leader in Egypt, revealing God's secrets to Pharaoh, and bringing nourishment and survival to his own family, the children of Abraham, the people of God, as well as to the people of Egypt. Joseph became the second most powerful man in the world in his day. He transitioned from being a shepherd in Canaan to a governmental official in Egypt, from one of the *least* significant places on earth to one of the *most* significant places on earth, all because of God's purpose in his life. Joseph's life fulfilled the prophecy given to Abraham, which spoke of God's people going into Egypt for a season and ultimately returning to the land of Canaan. Zaphenath-Paneah discovered and fulfilled his purpose in his generation. How can *we* learn and live God's purpose for us in *our* generation? Joseph's life can help us answer that question.

ESTABLISH IDENTITY

First, to fulfill our purpose in our generation, we must establish our identity. Our purpose flows from our identity, and if we do not understand who we are, we will never be able to become who God intended for us to be. Many have associated the "identity crisis" in our culture with Generation Z. This crisis threatens the God-given purposes of this new generation because our enemy knows that if he can confuse our identity, he can keep us from our purpose. During the temptation of Jesus in the wilderness, Lucifer attacked identity first. The first words he tempted Jesus with were, "If you are the Son of God...."[47] Even in Jesus's life, identity was key to purpose, so Satan tried to bring doubt regarding it. He does the same with each of us, first attacking our identity in order to move us away from our purpose.

Professor Dale Kuehne, author of *Sex and the iWorld: Rethinking Relationship Beyond an Age of Individualism*, gives an enlightening talk regarding purpose on Qideas.org. The site describes his talk by saying: "Modern culture has created a vacuum of purpose and identity. This has led to colossal confusion over why we exist and where we find meaning. Our mental health epidemic, the idolatry of sexuality, gender confusion and innumerable other challenges are rooted in a wrong view of human purpose, relationships and identity."[48]

Our Creator made us and knew each of us in our mother's womb. Our identity does not come from how many friends we have nor from how many "likes" we can generate on Instagram. Our identity comes from knowing who our Father is and from our identity as a son or daughter of the King. Still, a lack of earthly fathers has proven to make a big impact on Generation Z. This is one of the reasons I wrote the book *Father Cry*, in which I quoted David Blankenhorn, the founder of the Institute for American Values. Blankenhorn states that the trend of fatherlessness is "the most socially consequential family trend of our generation."[49] Furthermore, he "speaks for most Americans" when he says that more than 70 percent agree with the notion that "absence of fathers from the home is *the most significant* family or social problem facing America."[50]

Even in Jesus's life, identity was key to purpose, so Satan tried to bring doubt regarding it. He does the same with each of us, first attacking our identity in order to move us away from our purpose.

The deterioration of the family and the breakdown of inter-family relationships have put many Gen Zers in awkward associations with their earthly fathers. Many have no connection at all, and of those who do connect with their earthly fathers, many suffer through strained relationships at best. When you have a difficult relationship with your earthly father, you can find it difficult to identify correctly with your heavenly Father. Yet, your heart's cry to our heavenly Father will be heard, and He will help you find a clear identity as His son or daughter.[51]

The Bible states that Joseph was the favorite of his earthly father: "Now Israel loved Joseph more than any of his other sons, because he had been born to him in his old age; and he made an ornate robe for him," or as the King James Version says "a coat of many colors."[52] In that day, clothes represented ownership and favor, so Joseph's coat represented the love and favor of his father.

Clothes represent a lot to Gen Z, too. They spend a lot of money on them and pay a great deal of attention to them. In an ORU Chapel sermon series for Gen Z, I was talking about clothes and said, "I'm a baby boomer. You guys don't want me looking like Generation Z." Boy, was I wrong. To make a long story short, a few students took exception to the statement and asked if they could take me shopping (on my credit card, of course). They were eager to discover what would happen if a baby boomer willingly received fashion advice from a Gen Zer.

Needless to say, it was an adventure. I tried on some articles of clothing I had never seen before and some that gave me an all-too-familiar sense of my youth. (I am just glad no green crushed velvet leisure suits were involved! But that's a story for another time.) During the next message in the Gen Z series, I preached while wearing one of the outfits they had chosen, which the students *loved*. One of the items, the cool Calvin Klein sweatshirt, still hangs in my closet. But the socks with pizza slices all over them, the multicolored jean jacket, and the sailor-style pants were *quickly* gifted to incredibly grateful Gen Z students!

Through all the fun, my purpose in doing this was not just to get their attention—though I certainly did. It was also to prove to the students that we are not defined by what we wear on the outside. However, what we wear on the inside means *everything*. We see this throughout Scripture. God tells us that He has clothed us in the Spirit.[53] Paul says when we are in Christ, we have clothed ourselves with Him.[54]

Joseph's father gifted him a coat of many colors, and our heavenly Father has gifted you and me with the clothing of Jesus Christ and His righteousness. We are God's beloved, and *this* is our principal identity. When Joseph wore the coat his father had given to him, everybody knew that he had his father's favor. When we walk in Christ and stay clothed in His righteousness, the world will know that we have our Father's favor.

If we are going to fulfill our purpose, being a follower of Christ *must* become our principal identity. If we first think of ourselves in any other way, we will never accomplish what He has for us. When we awaken every morning, we can look in the mirror and notice: Yes, we have blonde hair or black hair, brown eyes or green eyes, yellow skin, white skin, or black skin, and any other characteristic, but most importantly, we are clothed in the righteousness of Jesus Christ. We are God's child *first*. And as a result, we are His favorite. Establishing our identity will lead to fulfilling our purpose.

SPEAK THE DREAM

As believers, we do not simply share a principal identity. We also share a general purpose. This purpose includes those things the Lord requires of us: "To act justly and to love mercy and to walk humbly with your God,"[55] and to pursue the ways He has predestined us to be conformed to the image of Jesus.[56] All of us are to do right, live right, and become more like Jesus.

Yet, our lives also have a specific purpose, which flows from our identity. When we begin to understand the Father's love, we can begin to dream His dreams for us.

Joseph started dreaming after receiving his coat of many colors. Those dreams began as the physical, nighttime ones, but they later birthed his life's vision. In his first dream, he saw what symbolized his brothers bowing down to him. In the second one, the symbolism included his brothers, mom, and dad bowing down to him. I used to preach that Joseph should have kept his mouth shut. I taught that you need not share everything that God is speaking to you all the time. Maybe that is still true, but as I researched this story further in light of purpose, I became less convinced of my original perspective. When Joseph voiced his vision and described his dreams, he initiated the process of his purpose. I strongly believe that when we speak our dream, we set into motion something supernatural.

Something happened when Ananias declared Paul's purpose.[57] Something happened when Samuel declared David's purpose.[58] Something happened when Jesus read the passage from Isaiah declaring His own purpose in the Nazareth synagogue.[59] And something happened to me when I was eleven years old—a young man standing at my grandfather's casket. When someone said, "Nobody will ever preach like that again," referring to my grandfather who was a Pentecostal pioneer and powerful preacher, something rose in my spirit that had obviously taken root in my heart. I responded confidently, "Yes, they will," knowing then that God had called me to fulfill that purpose. I was voicing the vision that started me on my journey. This verbalizing of the internal process released purpose in my life, and God began to move me toward that purpose. It is true—sometimes you have to *say* it to *start* it.

On May 13, 1900, Wilbur Wright wrote a letter to Octave Chanute, an experienced engineer and worldwide authority on flight at the time. He said: "For some years I have been afflicted with the belief that flight is possible to man. My disease has increased in severity, and I feel that it will soon cost me an increased amount of money, if not my life. I have been trying to arrange my affairs in such a way that I can devote my entire time for a few months to experiment in this field." Three years later, in 1903, the Wright brothers achieved the first manned flight.[60]

In an address he gave on May 25, 1961, President John F. Kennedy stated his goal of having the United States send a man to the moon by the end of the decade. Eight years later, in 1969, US astronaut Neil Armstrong stepped on the moon for the first time.[61] Speaking the dream and vision starts the process toward purpose in your life. As Joseph discovered, something significant happens in the supernatural when you declare your purpose and describe your dream.

ENDURE THE DIFFICULTY REQUIRED

Joseph may have understood God's purpose for his life from a young age, but his purpose-path was an unexpected one, to say the least. He was thrown into a pit, sold into slavery, made a servant in the house of Potiphar (an Egyptian leader), and thrown into jail where he remained for two years. Finally, he was brought before Pharaoh, interpreted the ruler's dreams, and ultimately was made the regent of all of Egypt, which made him second in command in the world at the time. This all happened during a thirteen-year span—from the time he heard God's voice as a young man until it all started to become a reality. As Friedrich Nietzsche said, "He who has a why to live for can bear almost any how."[62] Most people, like Joseph, endure a lot in order to see their God-given dream come to pass.

At ten years of age, Jim Carrey became absolutely enamored with acting. He immediately began to try many different things to break into show business, even sending his résumé to *The Carol Burnett Show*. But when Jim was fourteen years old, his father lost his job, and his entire family hit tough times. They moved into a Volkswagen van on a relative's lawn, and Carrey and his siblings were forced to get jobs working eight-hour shifts alongside their father after school.

At age fifteen, Carrey performed his first comedy routine onstage in a suit his mom made for him, and he totally bombed. But he did not abandon his dream. Around the age of sixteen, he dropped out of school and moved to Los Angeles, where he subsequently parked on Mulholland Drive every night and visualized his success. On one of those nights, in a moment of inspiration, he wrote himself a check for $10 million for "acting services rendered." Carrey dated the check for Thanksgiving 1995. Just before Thanksgiving of 1995, he had one of his largest paydays ever—a multimillion-dollar contract for *Dumb and Dumber*. He kept that old check in his wallet until his father died and placed it in his father's casket.[63] Jim Carrey endured and saw his dream come true.

Colonel Harland Sanders was fired from a variety of jobs before he started cooking chicken in his roadside Shell Oil gas station in 1930 when he was forty years old. During the Great Depression, his gas station did not have a restaurant, so he invited people into his home next door to feed them chicken. Over the next ten years, he perfected his secret recipe and pressure fryer cooking method for his famous fried chicken and moved onto larger locations. His chicken was even praised in the media by food critic Duncan Hines. Soon, however, an interstate was built, running through Louisville, Kentucky, and right where the Colonel's restaurant was located. The new highway redirected essential road traffic that his business had relied upon, and soon enough, the Colonel was forced to close down and retire, essentially broke.

Worried about how he would survive with his meager $105 monthly pension check, he set out to find restaurants that would franchise his secret recipe. He wanted a nickel for every piece of chicken sold. He drove around from place to place, sleeping in his car between stops. He was rejected a thousand times before finding his first partner, and after that partnership, the rest is history. Decades later, KFCs are everywhere and can account for a few extra pounds on people around the world because of Colonel Sanders' Kentucky Fried Chicken![64]

When God gives you a vision and a purpose, the road to fulfillment is not usually an easy one. Colonel Sanders, Jim Carrey, and Joseph would all attest to that. Their dreams came to pass, but they had to walk a difficult path to realization. Remember Joseph—he was thrown in a pit, sold, put in jail, lied about, cheated, and forgotten, but God kept bringing him through. To fulfill your purpose, you have to make up your mind that you will do whatever is required to experience its fulfillment. And God will help you by His grace. Paul encouraged the Galatian believers when he wrote, "Let us not become weary in doing good, for at the proper time we will reap a harvest if we do not give up."[65]

REFUSE TO COMPROMISE

Scripture clearly reveals that while Joseph was working in Potiphar's house, he encountered an interesting and tempting situation. Potiphar's wife developed a romantic attraction for Joseph and tried multiple times to seduce him into sleeping with her. One day, while she was attempting to entice him, Joseph escaped, leaving his slave coat in her hands. God says to this generation in the same way: "Flee from sexual immorality"[66] and "Flee the evil desires of youth and pursue righteousness."[67] To fulfill your destiny, you must resolve not to sacrifice it on an altar for a fleeting moment of good feelings. As Joseph's life proves, when you keep your integrity, you will keep your favor.

To fulfill your purpose, you have to make up your mind that you will do whatever is required to experience its fulfillment. And God will help you by His grace.

PREPARE FOR THE POSSIBILITIES

In verse after verse, we read that Joseph was prepared to excel in whatever situation he was placed. When his time came, he was ready to interpret dreams. Why? Because he himself was one of the original dreamers. Joseph learned about dreams firsthand by witnessing how his dreams came to pass. When Pharaoh had a dream that he could not explain, Joseph told him exactly what it meant. He was ready for the opportunities that came his way. You too must prepare for the possibilities, so that when the doors open, you can step confidently through them and do what God has called you to do. Your purpose requires preparation.

PARDON THE PAIN

Perhaps the greatest threat to fulfilling your purpose will be how others respond to you. That is why we must allow this truth to be deeply ingrained in our hearts: *Forgiveness is a purpose propellant.* Joseph, when mistreated and betrayed by his brothers, forgave them. When he had children in Egypt, he named the first one "Ephraim," meaning "double fruitfulness,"[68] and the second one "Manasseh," meaning "who makes to forget."[69] Joseph let go of what would keep him from fulfilling his purpose. He pardoned the pain others had caused him, and it propelled him into his purpose.

FOCUS ON THE FINISH

The story of Zaphenath-Paneah reminds us not to forget God's endgame related to our purpose. The fact is that fulfilling your purpose is not ultimately about you; it is about God, and it is about others. Near the end of his life, "Joseph made the Israelites swear an oath and said, 'God will surely come to your aid, and then you must carry my bones up from this place.'"[70] The New Testament writer records, "By faith Joseph, when his end was near, spoke about the exodus of the Israelites from Egypt and gave instructions concerning the burial of his bones."[71]

During my afternoon shopping excursion with the students, I experienced a moment that I will not soon forget, one that I certainly was not expecting. There in that Urban Outfitters dressing room in Tulsa's Brookside District, as I was lacing up lf as a young adult. The Lord reminded me of feelings I felt as a seventeen- to twenty-year-old. He stopped me as I was putting on that shoe and spoke these words to my spirit: "Don't forget what this felt like, Billy. Remember the uncertainty you had and tell the students to relax. Tell them that God's got them and remind them to never forget whose clothes they're wearing."

Friends, if you are in Christ, please know today you are clothed with His righteousness and with the Father's love. So, *dream*. Let the security of knowing that God has you allow you to dream and dream *big*. When you are sure you are dreaming God's dream—and it has been confirmed two or three ways in your heart—speak it out and let God activate the purpose-process of your life. Then, like Zaphenath-Paneah, when the path gets tough, remember whose you are. Never forget that God has you.

Never forget that God has you.

Sure, physical clothes are okay but do not allow yourself to get tied up in what will not endure. Go above the superficial. Let nothing that has happened to you for one moment speak to your identity. Go above your past. Wherever you come from— you *can* rise higher. You can proclaim that you are a child of the living God. Your spiritual brother is Jesus Christ. You are clothed in God's righteousness. You have been washed in the blood. You have been set upon a rock. Your future is secure. Heaven is your home. Your righteousness is in Christ Jesus, and you *will* fulfill your purpose, by the grace of God.

CHAPTER THREE
A GENERATION BORN TO WORSHIP: ZADOK

Nelson Mandela said, "Sometimes, it falls upon a generation to be great. You can be that great generation."[72] When I hear this statement, I cannot help but think of Generation Z. They are a generation that, in my opinion, will become the most impactful generation in the history of the world. But to further understand Gen Z, we must first take a look at those who came before them, those who laid the foundation they now stand upon.

Sociologists have studied generations for years, giving them titles and revealing characteristics that help us to understand them in a broad context. In 1998, Tom Brokaw wrote a book called *The Greatest Generation*, which coined the generation's title and set out to profile those Americans born between 1901 and 1927.[73] Although I believe that Gen Z will be the greatest generation, Brokaw's greatest generation indeed had a great impact on the world. This amazing generation (two of them were my grandparents) endured and won World War I. Then, between 1928 and 1945, the "silent generation" was born. They grew up during the Great Depression and World War II, which taught them to make the most of what they had. This *Leave It to Beaver* generation believed in the nuclear family, held moral values high, and birthed the largest generation in the history of America until now, the "baby boomer generation." I am a part of this group, born between 1946 and 1964. Boomers were influenced by the Cold War, the Kennedy assassination, the first moon landing, and Woodstock, a music festival often credited with sparking the sex and drug revolution in America.

Baby boomers were followed by "Generation X." These were people born in America between 1965 and 1980. They saw the end of the Cold War, the first personal computer, and the Challenger explosion. They also watched divorce become rampant in America, ravaging many families, and in many instances, their own hearts. Most have called the generation that follows Generation X the "millennials," while some have labeled it "Generation Y." This group was born between 1981 and 1995. They saw the arrival of the new millennium, observed the Iraq War, and rode the first wave of social media, video games, and reality television. All of these prior generations precede this new generation: "Generation Z" or "Gen Z," as I call them throughout this book. They are now officially the largest generation in the United States.[74]

Gen Z has been known by other names, including "iGeneration," "Gen Tech," and "Post-Millennials," but according to Michael Dimock, president of the Pew Research Center, "While there is no scientific process for deciding when a name has stuck, the momentum is clearly behind Gen Z."[75] According to Pew Research Center, "Gen Z" has become the leading defining term, so much so that both the Merriam-Webster and Oxford dictionaries now have entries for the word.[76] I believe that is because whereas some of the generational labels are Western or American, "Gen Z" is a global phenomenon with connectivity across nations and similar characteristics that supersede geography. In a *New York Times* article, one young girl explains the pull toward the title in this way: "Gen Z is the final generation of the 1900s, and a generational title using the last letter in the alphabet seems fitting."[77] Others state that it only makes sense since the two previous generations are known as Generation X and Generation Y.[78] Whatever the reason, or perhaps *reasons*, it is clear that the term "Gen Z" is here to stay.

It is vital to remember that generations are not simply something concocted by sociologists. They are actually designed by God Himself. When we read His Word, we find that God has worked in and through generations since the beginning of time. King Solomon observed, "Generations come and generations go, but the earth remains forever."[79]

> **It is vital to remember that generations are not simply something concocted by sociologists. They are actually designed by God Himself.**

My primary goal in writing this book is to help us understand Gen Z's unique place in history and the amazing opportunity Gen Zers have to make an impact on our world as the rest of us walk alongside and champion them. If you are a Gen Zer, be encouraged today that you have been chosen to live in one of the most defining moments in all of history. You were born for such a time as *this*!

So, Who Is Gen Z?

We have talked some about the events that have shaped the lives of this distinct generation and how they view purpose and work, but now, let's look deeper. Who are these young people we are interacting with every day? If you are a Gen Zer, how do people view you and what does that mean for the future of society? As mentioned before, Gen Z was born into a world larger than it has ever been. The graph below shows this.

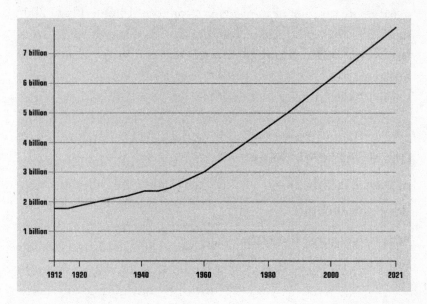

Fig. 3.1: World population graph[80]

In the early 1900s, the population growth curve appeared somewhat flat. Then, around the time of World War II, through the baby boomer generation and beyond, the curve escalated exponentially. Nearing the end of 2020, there were approximately 7.8 billion people in the world.[81] Though this is a great opportunity for Gen Z, it also presents an immense challenge for them as they have more people, technology, social issues, and threats to their safety to deal with than ever before.

In 2001, Gen Z experienced 9/11, which signaled the invasion of global terrorism into their world. They have grown up most of their lives not knowing if they might go into a concert, mall, or school and face a terrorist attack that could take their lives. In 2007, they saw what some consider to be one of the greatest inventions of their generation: the iPhone. From 2007 to 2009, they and their families lived through the Great Recession, which brought a huge correction to their family finances.

In 2008, America elected its first-ever Black president, a grand, historic moment in our nation. In 2015–2016, the Obergefell vs. Hodges case was tried at the Supreme Court, and the ultimate decision was made to legalize gay marriage across the United States. Then, in 2016, Donald Trump was elected president of the US, navigating our country's way to economic stability and facing head-on issues such as COVID-19, which in many ways brought Americans' lives to a sudden halt at the start of 2020.

One of the "definitions" of Gen Z is that they defy one unified descriptor, and they are quite proud of that.

Still, while we can identify many of the factors and events they have experienced, defining Generation Z is not easy. In fact, one of the "definitions" of Gen Z is that they defy one unified descriptor, and they are quite proud of that. More about that later, but first, let's look at some specific terms others have used to describe Gen Z. *Gen Z @ Work* is an interesting book, written by the father-son duo of David and Jonah Stillman.[82] This book caught my attention because it includes the perspectives of both a Gen X father, David, and his Gen Z, eighteen-year-old (at the time) son, Jonah.

The authors describe Gen Z as "phigital," meaning that to them, no difference exists between the digital and physical worlds. They also call them "hyper-custom" because of their generation's unique opportunity to customize everything. Rarely do Gen Zers buy full music albums; instead, they download individual songs from a variety of bands and artists, creating a customized playlist. Another word they use to describe Gen Z is "realistic." Because they have lived through the recession of 2007–8, they seem to understand that life is not always easy, and that to excel, they must feel and respond well to that pressure.

The Stillmans call Gen Z "weconomists," meaning they believe that their generation will work together throughout their lifetimes to help economic scale. They discuss their obsession with FOMO (fear of missing out), which is proven by the fact that Gen Z is estimated to check social media every twenty seconds because they are afraid they will miss something important. The authors also call Gen Z the "DIY" generation because they tend to believe they can do just about anything themselves—as long as there is a YouTube video to show them how. And finally, Gen Z is called a "driven" generation. They are a people proud of their accomplishments and intently set on succeeding. [83]

In a recent series of the *World Impact with Billy Wilson* television show, we focused specifically on this distinctive generation.[84] During one episode, our ORU spiritual life directors went beyond statistics and directly to the source, asking several Gen Z students how *they* viewed their culture. Here are some things they said.

- They are obsessed with people at the top of their game — people like Beyoncé, the Kardashian/Jenner clan, LeBron James, and Serena Williams. Why? Because "They're number one, and we all want to be number one in something."
- They are focused on fashion — how clothes feel and how they make them look.
- Social media has "taken over" and become a large part of who they are. It adds both positives and negatives to their lives.
- In a negative sense, social media serves as a tool for "constant comparison to other people." According to one student, "Everyone puts their highlight reel on there [social media]. So, when you're comparing your everyday life to someone's best moments, you're going to feel empty and unfulfilled."
- In a positive sense, the students appreciate the influence social media has on their faith. "All of our pastors are on our phones and laptops now. We don't actually have to go to church to feel like we're there. God is all on YouTube and Instagram. You see influencers. . . talk about their relationship with Him," one of them explained.

Some of the words I would use to describe this wonderful group of people I get the privilege of spending most of my days with are these:
- Technologically advanced
- Industrious
- Entrepreneurial
- Globally connected

- Passionate about changing the world
- Pragmatic
- Multiracial and accepting of all
- Individualistic

All of these definitions describe Gen Z from a general perspective. Now, I want to focus heavily on explaining the DNA of Gen Z from a spiritual stance. As a college president serving in a living laboratory of Gen Zers, I have found them to be a "no-frills" generation in the arena of spirituality. They want truth, clarity, purpose, authenticity, and practicality. They long for both purity and God's presence. This has brought what I believe has been and will continue to be a new restoration of the priesthood of the believer—individuals who *truly* know how to connect with God intimately and authentically.

[I have found them to be a "no-frills" generation in the arena of spirituality. They want truth, clarity, purpose, authenticity, and practicality.]]

A Unique Individuality

One of the qualities on my list—individuality—is the primary trait I believe will impact the way Gen Z (and ultimately the world) connects with God. Millennials, who came directly before Gen Zers, were known to travel in groups. At ORU, we discovered that if we could influence the *friends* of the millennial, we could usually influence the *millennial.* But with Gen Z, influence is different. We have found that while they *do* have friends and are influenced by them to a degree, they also recognize their individuality and understand that their choices count. That is why in class, though they enjoy working on group projects, they also want their own grade—especially if they are better at the subject than the rest. They want to excel, to stand out, and to be viewed as unique individuals. I believe God will use this trait in Gen Zers to connect with the truth that each person has access to God.

Throughout this book, we are focusing on people in Scripture whose names begin with "Z" to help us identify what God is doing and wants to do in Generation Z. In this chapter, I want to focus on a man who was a true worshipper. I have never heard a sermon on him, but as we talk about Gen Z becoming a new generation of worshippers, I think he serves as a great example.

ZADOK

The name "Zadok" means "righteous," "just," or "justified." Zadok came from a family of priests, and he ultimately became the high priest though he was not in the direct lineage to do so when he began his priestly ministry. In his lifetime, God favored and positioned him in such a way that he began a whole new generation of priests.

Zadok lived during the time of King David. He helped bring the Ark of the Covenant to Jerusalem[85] and a new order of worship for both David's house and the tabernacle, which was set up on Mount Zion before the temple was built.[86] He fled with David, along with Abiathar—the other high priest of Israel at the time—when the king's son Absalom started a rebellion against his father. When David left Jerusalem, "The whole countryside wept aloud as all the people passed by . . ."[87] Zadok, Abiathar, and the Levites were carrying the Ark of the Covenant in the procession with David—that is, until David commanded them to return it to Jerusalem. At a time when the nation of Israel was drawn to Absalom's charm and charisma, Zadok remained faithful to the king whom God anointed—King David. In fact, he remained devoted to David throughout his entire reign.

Following David's reign, Zadok remained loyal to the successor—the king's son Solomon—chosen by both David and God. When Adonijah (another of David's sons with Absalom's charm and charisma) attempted to usurp Solomon's throne, Abiathar went with David's general, Joab, to anoint Adonijah king, but David sent Zadok to anoint Solomon first, and he went willingly.[88] Because of this dedication to the true, chosen king, Zadok eventually became the sole high priest of Israel under the rule and ministry of King Solomon.[89] Through his devotion, he established a new line of priests, who were also known for their favor before God and man and for their purity and loyalty to the *real* king.

Zadok and his successors were so favored by God that when the Lord downloaded the plans and process for the new temple and priesthood to the exiled prophet Ezekiel, Zadok was mentioned: "and the room facing north is for the priests who guard the altar. These are the sons of Zadok, who are the only Levites who may draw near to the LORD to minister before him."[90] Later, Ezekiel was told, "'But the Levitical priests, who are descendants of Zadok and who guarded my sanctuary when the Israelites went astray from me, are to come near to minister before me; they are to stand before me to offer sacrifices of fat and blood,' declares the Sovereign LORD."[91]

Zadok, because he was loyal and righteous before God, established a new line of priestly order recognized by God, revealed to Ezekiel, and favored throughout time and eternity. Because he was a true worshipper of the true King, he changed the lives of the generations that would follow him.

Zadok revolutionized worship in his day, and I believe Gen Z is revolutionizing worship in the twenty-first century. Let me explain how. Zadok would not go with Absalom or Adonijah, who were both good-looking, full of charisma, and seemed to be "the thing" of their day. He understood that the king exalted by God is the one who deserves loyalty. As believers in the twenty-first century, we know that our devotion belongs not to King David, the ancient earthly king, but to Jesus Christ, the Son of the living God, who has now been exalted as the King of Kings and Lord of Lords.

Gen Z gets this. It does not matter so much to them who is on the stage, what their name is, how they are dressed, or many times, even how they play music. Of course, they like it when people dress cool and sound good, but I have noticed something unique about this generation. They can, for the most part, get past the personal charisma of the ones leading worship and focus their loyalty on the One who is over all— Jesus Christ. So, if an incredibly anointed group came through town and led a great service, but the next week, they backslid, the Gen Z crowd would likely not be as disturbed as many in previous generations would have been. Why? Because they were not worshipping those people to begin with. They were worshipping the King of heaven.

The firm conviction of my heart is that because of this innate ability to focus on what matters and their individualistic desire for their *own* relationship with the King, Gen Z will establish a new priesthood of worshippers in the earth—ones who, like the line of Zadok, are favored both now and throughout eternity. Let's identify and explore some of the qualities this new priesthood must possess.

Because of this innate ability to focus on what matters and their individualistic desire for their *own* relationship with the King, Gen Z will establish a new priesthood of worshippers in the earth.

WORSHIP MUST BE PURE

God is calling for purity in worship. The psalmist posed the question, "Who may ascend the mountain of the LORD? Who may stand in his holy place?" then responded, "The one who has clean hands and a pure heart, who does not trust in an idol or swear by a false god. They will receive blessing from the LORD and vindication from God their Savior. Such is the generation of those who seek him, who seek your face, God of Jacob."[92]

One of the words you hear most often from this *now* generation is "authenticity," which I like to call "integrity of heart." They want people and things that are real. I often challenge them to understand the difference between *perceived* authenticity and *real* authenticity since discernment is required to tell when authenticity is genuine and not for the sake of gain. And genuine authenticity is something this generation longs for. That is why we must ensure our worship is authentic, pure, and filled with an integrity of heart.

I often joke with our students that I am from "Generation O," which stands for "Generation Old." But what I love about them is although they *did* enjoy dressing me for a week, they do not *actually* want me to try to be like them. They want me to be authentic, to be who God made *me* to be. Stephen Charnock, an English Presbyterian clergyman in the seventeenth century, said, "Without the heart it is no worship; it is a stage play; an acting a part without being that person really which is acted by us: a hypocrite, in the notion of the world, is a stage-player ... We may truly be said to worship God though we lack perfection; but we cannot be said to worship Him if we lack sincerity."[93]

Unlike Zadok's pure, authentic worship, we find throughout Scripture several stories of people who feigned the authentic worship of God. Faking authenticity brings death. Sometimes this is physical death, but inauthentic worship always brings spiritual death. For instance, Nadab and Abihu, sons of Moses's brother Aaron, were in line to become the "Zadoks" of their day, but they made a destiny-altering mistake. After watching God rain down fire on the altar as God's people worshipped Him, they decided to create their own, strange fire before God—not fire from the altar of the burnt offering. When they used this fake fire, He smote them with His *real* fire, and they died.[94] In the same way, hypocritical, inauthentic worship is deadly to both the church and the believer. Though it might not kill the person physically, the spiritual death is excruciating.

Another example is Judas, the disciple who betrayed Jesus with a kiss. The word "worship" is translated from the Greek word *proskuneo*, which means "to make obeisance," "to do reverence to," "to awe," "to express devotion," "to express honor of God's worthiness," "worth-ship," or my favorite definition—"to kiss."[95]

Eugene Peterson paraphrased Psalm 2:11–12 in this way: "Worship GOD in adoring embrace, Celebrate in trembling awe. Kiss Messiah!" (MSG). Worship is spiritually kissing God, expressing the deepest intimacies of our hearts toward Him. Yet, in the garden of Gethsemane, Judas used this holy symbol of worship, intimacy, and desire for God to betray His Son. Jesus asked him, "Judas, are you betraying the Son of Man with a kiss?"[96] Because of this betrayal, Judas experienced the dark, sad emptiness that comes from faking it. Death ensued.

Ananias and Sapphira also learned that insincere worship brings death. After a Levite named Barnabas sold a piece of land and gave all the money to the apostles for the spreading of the gospel,[97] Ananias and Sapphira decided to sell some of their property too and give money to the apostles. Instead of following Barnabas' example of pure worship in giving, they lied about the amount they received for the land and kept some of the profit for themselves.[98] Their goal was an insincere one—to be recognized for their charity. This was meant to be their "selfie moment"—the moment that would cause their Instagram and Snapchat stories to be the talk of the town because they were giving a generous gift to Jesus's disciples. That's "holy," right? Not when done with insincerity, as we see in the rest of the story.

When Ananias gave the money, Peter discerned the hypocrisy and inauthenticity of the moment and asked, "Ananias, why have you lied to the Holy Spirit?"[99] Immediately, Ananias fell over dead. Sapphira came in next, and Peter asked her,

"Is this the amount you sold the land for?"[100] She said, "yes," and immediately fell over dead, too. God's response to this inauthentic, impure, self-focused kind of worship was instant death. May those who fake worship to gain followers or increase album sales take note. God is not playing games in this area, and inauthenticity will bring death.

The narrative of Ananias and Sapphira ends with a phrase that can be easily overlooked. It says that the *young* generation carried them [Ananias and Sapphira] out. I see this as a picture of what God wants Gen Z to do in the body of Christ today. God desires for this generation to carry the impurity and insincerity out of His church. This generation knows that "faking it" is deadly. They also know that purity, authenticity, and integrity matter to God. In God's presence, we are to be ourselves, but we're to be our *best* selves—and kiss Jesus in *pure* devotion.

The *World Impact* team asked Gen Z how they viewed worship, and their responses proved that they do indeed see the need for purity and authenticity. The director of ORU's worship center said, "Worship goes beyond music . . . [it] is a lifestyle, and it's something that influences how we think, what we say, how we act." A worship leader for ORU Live responded, "When you're on stage, people can see your authentic worship. They will notice that 'Hey, this guy really knows Jesus. This guy really knows what he is talking about . . . .' When you've been somewhere, they know . . . You can't bring people to where you've never been." [101] Yes. *This* is authenticity.

Later in the show, ORU's spiritual life directors asked several students how they felt their generation identified worship. Here are a few of their responses:

- "We like worship services and worship songs . . . But I think that (worship is) a life that is surrendered to Christ . . . ."
- "The person who is in charge of leading worship plays a very big part in how worship goes . . .. Their life outside of worshipping and leading is a very big factor."
- "What I think makes that atmosphere possible is the lifestyle coming into the atmosphere—the heart posture coming into the atmosphere."

They get it. Worship is more than songs. Worship is loyalty to the King, whether in a church service or a classroom, at work, or in the grocery store. We are called to live *sincere* lives of worship that purely honor Him. Generation Z will not settle for merely *acting* like they are worshipping God when their hearts are far from Him. Instead, they will authentically embrace God. They will live like Zadok—loyal to the one true King.

Gen Z loves technology, yet they also crave face-to-face interaction, mentorship, and connection.

WORSHIP MUST BE PERSONAL

Gen Z loves technology, yet they also crave face-to-face interaction, mentorship, and connection. That is exactly what worship is— FaceTime with Jesus.

In John's narrative of the woman at the well, we read the following exchange:

"Sir," the woman said, "I can see that you are a prophet. Our ancestors worshiped on this mountain, but you Jews claim that the place where we must worship is in Jerusalem."

"Woman," Jesus replied, "believe me, a time is coming when you will worship the Father neither on this mountain nor in Jerusalem. You Samaritans worship what you do not know; we worship what we do know, for salvation is from the Jews. Yet a time is coming and has now come when the true worshipers will worship the Father in the Spirit and in truth, for they are the kind of worshipers the Father seeks. God is spirit, and his worshipers must worship in the Spirit and in truth."[102]

Jesus established that worship is not geographical but *geo-personal*. He told this woman that worship is about knowing God personally—not about worshipping in one specific place. Worship doesn't have to *only* happen in church; it can happen wherever you are on Planet Earth. It occurs whenever you embrace heaven, open your heart, and proclaim the goodness of God. When we worship Him in Spirit and in truth, we are worshipping from our deepest person in the purity of God's truth. It is not just about a four-song setlist at the beginning of a church service, the newest worship album by your favorite artist, or a summer spent on a mission trip. Gen Z understands that. They are seeking *new* revelation and revival that only comes from worship that is personal.

Zadok's life proved what God can do in the life of someone who understands this type of worship. Throughout his story, we see time and time again that he was a true worshipper, not confined to a place but only to a person, the *true* King. Whether he was outside of Jerusalem or formally ordering the worship in the tabernacle, his worship remained deeply personal.

WORSHIP MUST BE PASSIONATE

The final quality that Gen Z's worship revolution must possess—and, I believe, already possesses—is passion. The psalmist said, "I will praise you, LORD, with all my heart..."[103] To truly worship God, our whole being must be involved—physical, emotional, and spiritual.

A. W. Tozer said, "I can safely say, on the authority of all that is revealed in the Word of God, that any man or woman on this earth who is bored and turned off by worship is not ready for heaven."[104]

Charles Spurgeon wrote, "I believe that in public worship we should do well to be bound by no human rules and constrained by no stereotyped order."[105]

Jonathan Edwards, known as one of the chief fathers of the First Great Awakening in America, had seen the American church transition from a stiff, cerebral, dead group of people into what he called "the people of God on fire" experiencing visceral religion. Ultimately, he came to believe that if you did not *feel* something, you probably did not know the living God. He said, "Who will deny that true religion consists, in a great measure, in vigorous and lively actings of the inclination and will of the soul, or the fervent exercises of the heart? That religion which God requires, and will accept, does not consist in weak, dull, and lifeless wishes, raising us but a little above a state of indifference."[106]

What Gen Z seems to intuitively understand about worship is what I believe will revolutionize it for generations to come.

Just as Zadok established worship that was pure, personal, and passionate, so will Generation Z. Like him, they will establish a new priesthood, one that is *pure* and authentic—not giving way to hypocrisy. They will pursue *personal* worship, which seeks to know God individually, in the most intimate of ways. They will make it about a lifestyle—not a location. And finally, they will recognize the worthiness of the Father to inhabit our entire lives in *passionate* worship. Zadok was willing to risk his whole life in honor and loyalty to the King. Because of this, he ended his life having served the purpose of God for his generation and having influenced generations to come. What will be said of our worship? For Gen Z, I believe it will be said that their worship will change the course of history.

CHAPTER FOUR

A GENERATION BORN FOR THE SPIRIT: ZECHARIAH AND ZERUBBABEL

n January of 2013, I arrived at a hotel room in the Dallas/ Fort Worth airport for what would ultimately become a defining moment in my life. The next morning, I was scheduled to meet with the presidential search committee of Oral Roberts University. At the time, I was serving as vice-chair of the ORU Board of Trustees and was honored to do so. The succession plan was that I was to become board chair over the next years to assure continuance. This sounded good to me. Yet, I knew deep in my spirit that God might have something else in mind. My name had surfaced in discussions for the presidency a couple of times, but I had preferred that the committee find someone else, which would allow us to continue with the succession plan. The search committee ultimately requested that I allow my name to be in the process and asked me to submit materials to them as well as meet them for an interview. I arrived in Dallas to facilitate this request.

The night before the meeting, my wife, Lisa, had an interesting and difficult dream. She called me early that morning, and I immediately discerned that her dream was a call to prayer. As I knelt by my hotel bed and prayed for what lay ahead of me that day, including further discernment regarding Lisa's dream, the Holy Spirit fell on me, and I prayed in tongues for a long time. This was not unusual as I pray in tongues most days of my life, but in this case, I received the interpretation of my prayer language. It was a very powerful message and a dramatic moment for me. I found myself crying, nearly uncontrollably. My inner man had been touched deeply, but the tears were because I knew at that moment what both God and the search committee were about to ask me to do. In my spirit, I understood that I would be asked to serve as president of ORU, and I knew that God wanted me to accept it.

With tears running down my face, I sat in the middle of the bed and conversed with my heavenly Father. I knew that serving as president of any university is not an easy job, and because of my position on the ORU Board of Trustees, I also knew some of the difficulties a new president would face. To be honest, I was not sure I wanted to assume that responsibility—not because I would not be honored by the request (I certainly would be), but because I simply thought it too big a job for me. "God, I don't think I can do this," I finally muttered through my tears. I then began to explain my reasons with one primary explanation, as if it would get me out of the job: "I know that whoever is president will have to raise between eight and ten million dollars per year just to stay in the black and keep the university's doors open. And God, You know that I have *never* raised that much money in my entire life, much less in one year."

It was a tough moment for me. I had to admit that I was not up for this. Yet, the Holy Spirit, in His ever-comforting way, responded, "Don't worry about it. I've got that part under control. Just say yes." No insight was given; no strategy was downloaded—just a simple phrase that brought immense peace. "I've got it; just say yes." The interview went well, God's grace was present, and ultimately the search committee offered me the presidency. I accepted though, admittedly, I was still concerned about the fundraising aspect of the job.

When I look back on that moment, I am reminded of the words of the prophet Zechariah. God speaks through him to say, "Not by might nor by power, but by my Spirit."[107]

Essentially, that is what I felt the Holy Spirit impress upon me that day. He told me that all would be okay—not because I would suddenly become great at fundraising, not because I was so smart, not even because I had special favor. He told me that it would be okay because of His power and His ability.

Thus far, God has *more* than kept His word to me. Since that tearful moment in Dallas, ORU has met the mark and remained in the black every year during my presidency. Actually, we have not just *hit* the mark; we have *exceeded* it, raising fifteen to sixteen million dollars every single year. Yes, we have worked hard. Yes, we have projected a bold vision. Yes, we have met with people all over the world, inviting them to move from success to significance by investing in a new generation, and yes, we have overcome significant challenges. But most importantly, we have seen the impossible become possible by God's supernatural help for both the university and our donors. The fact is that God does what man cannot do when we obey Him. His Word and His work travel on the wind of His Spirit. It is not by human power nor might but by His Spirit that His will is accomplished in the earth. Only by His Spirit has His provision come to ORU.

The fact is that God does what man cannot do when we obey Him.

Secondhand Spirituality

In my daily encounters with Gen Z, I have witnessed a mammoth desire among them to learn the ways of the Spirit. Many of their generational markers and characteristics position them to be part of a fresh moving of the Holy Spirit. What many people consider negative can work to the positive when committed to the Spirit.

Gen Z is often called the "iGeneration" because they are incredibly individualistic. Although this can be negative concerning community and their commitment to the body of Christ, it can also be a powerful opportunity for the Holy Spirit to work. Because experiences and products have been customized for them since they were children, I do not believe that Gen Z will settle for a secondhand experience with the Spirit. They want their *own* encounter and their *own* story. It is not enough for them to hear of what God has done for others — though they love firsthand accounts. Rather, they want to experience Him personally. It is great to hear about miracles, but they want to see miracles in their *own* lives. It is wonderful to hear about God's financial supply, but they want to know the answer to the question "What about my need *now*?" This passion for the personal will continue to position them to encounter the Holy Spirit. On the day of Pentecost, the Holy Spirit visited the corporate Church, but He also visited individuals. A flame appeared on each head, and every individual in the crowd of 120 emerged to tell of their very own, personal encounter with God.[108] Their story changed the world!

Gen Z not only craves individuality; they also crave immediacy. They want what they want when they want it. This obviously can be negative when it leads to impatience and an attempt to make things happen by their own power and strength. "Hagars" and "Ishmaels" are the result when we do not learn how to wait on God for His absolute best. However, this longing for the *now* also encourages them to crave immediate access to God. They do not need to wait until Sunday to hear from the Spirit or see God work. He is present in the *now* and able to quench their longing for Him at any moment. When this desire is turned to the Father, the result will be 24/7 encounters with the Holy Spirit.

Global connectivity and passion are other significant markers of this generation. Because of media and travel, they have grown up more as global citizens than as local citizens. In fact, Generation Z is not just a Western phenomenon or grouping; rather, many of the same characteristics of this new generation cross geopolitical and cultural borders. The longing to make a difference on a global scale is palpable in this generation. This generational passion for the world will lead to a fresh dependency on the Holy Spirit, who will empower them to find global significance beyond their own strength or ability.

This passion for uncomplicated, authentic, not overly-processed spirituality is exactly one of the reasons we will see a fresh outpouring of the Holy Spirit in our times and will also witness a return to the beauty of simple, *real* Christianity.

Finally, as noted earlier, authenticity is critical. Gen Z wants what is real, tangible, verifiable, and authentic. Megan Goodwin, a Mellon Postdoctoral Fellow in Creative and Innovative Pedagogy in Humanities and a lecturer in religious studies at Bates College in Lewiston, Maine, explains Gen Z's yearning for genuineness in a helpful way. She says, "What Gen Z wants is a story they can believe in, told in a way that is stripped of over-complicated production techniques and isn't overly processed."[109] My experience has been that she is right. This passion for uncomplicated, authentic, not overly-processed spirituality is exactly one of the reasons we will see a fresh outpouring of the Holy Spirit in our times and will also witness a return to the beauty of simple, *real* Christianity.

Challenges

Gen Z is living in a fully post-modern world. Absolutes have collapsed, and every person has become right in his or her own eyes. Our world is now fluid, and as Thomas Friedman stated in his oft-quoted book, *The World Is Flat*.[110] It is a world where the givens have given way. Those things that were once thought stable by the Greatest Generation — and even by baby boomers, in many ways — have eroded to such an extent that this generation has few markers they feel are certain or absolute.

Sociologists and scholars say that the West has become "post-Christian" because of its influences.[111] I do not necessarily agree with this philosophy, but it is stated repeatedly by members of the press and politicians alike. Amid the vacuum created in post-modernity and post-Christian thinking, several options have emerged. Pluralism teaches that there are many ways to God and whatever way you choose is acceptable because all spiritual roads end at the same destination. Pluralism and inclusivity are pervasive philosophies in the twenty-first century, and new generations have been deeply affected by these influences. I am not sure we could overstate this issue as even committed Christ-followers struggle against these forces.

Brooke Hempell, Barna senior vice president of research, states, "Gen Z has a highly inclusive and individualistic worldview and moral code."[112] To a secular Gen Z youth, one of the greatest evils that could be espoused is to exclude someone for any reason. Exclusion or exclusivity of any kind is seen as morally wrong and evil in and of itself. Pluralism and this inclusive mindset contradict the claims of Jesus as the only way, truth, and life. The declaration that the only way to be saved is through a personal relationship with Jesus Christ is difficult for many Gen Z youth to fully embrace since this would mean exclusion instead of the inclusion they have been taught their entire lives.

The same tension emerges with Gen Z when the concepts of hell and heaven are preached or taught. How could God exclude anyone? If exclusion is evil as most have been led to believe, then how could a good God do this? Christ-following, Gen Z youth will be required to break from their generational code to stand for Scripture and the truth demanded by the uniqueness of Jesus Christ.

Not only has the philosophy of pluralism and inclusion infiltrated the psyche of an entire generation, but an increasing number in this generation are choosing not even to pursue a way to God. One of the fastest-growing religious groups in America is what scholars call the "nones"—those who claim to be non-affiliated with any religion.[113] These people are not religiously pluralistic—they are simply not religious. A Barna Research poll conducted in 2018 reports that 13 percent of American thirteen- to eighteen-year-olds consider themselves atheists, as compared to 6 percent of the total population. The young people's rate is more than *double* that of the national rate![114] In their book *Faith for Exiles*, authors David Kinnaman and Mark Matlock say that only 10 percent of young Christians are what they call "resilient disciples," meaning their faith is "vibrant and robust." They further categorize these "resilient disciples" in this way: "Christians who (1) attend church at least monthly and engage with their church more than just attending worship services; (2) trust firmly in the authority of the Bible; (3) are committed to Jesus personally and affirm he was crucified and raised from the dead to conquer sin and death; and (4) express desire to transform the broader society as an outcome of their faith."[115]

In addition to the increasing trend to believe in either everything or nothing, Gen Z is also under other extreme spiritual pressures. One of their greatest challenges is pornography. According to James Emery White, 70 percent of all eighteen- to thirty-four-year-olds say they are regular viewers of porn, and the average age they began viewing is eleven years old. In 2014, one porn site alone had more than 15.35 billion visits![116] And yes—there are only 7.8 billion people in the world.[117] Many times, when I talk personally with young men who struggle with this, many of them say the battle began when they were young, between the ages of eight and twelve. (Young ladies struggle, too, but I tend to have my wife talk to them about this subject.) Several of them credit their early beginnings to the fact that they were "babysat" by technology, went too far too fast, and found themselves trapped.

The prince of darkness knows the potential of every single Generation Z individual on the planet, and he plans to thwart that potential in any way possible. This generation is positioned and poised to impact the world in greater ways than most any people group in the history of humankind, so we should expect that Satan would attempt to protect his kingdom by blunting their spiritual effectiveness, enveloping them in confusion, challenging their identity, and drawing them away from the power of the Holy Spirit. The greater the struggle endured, the greater the victory enjoyed. The deep spiritual battle this generation encounters every day requires supernatural help and assistance. These multilayered, multidimensional inner struggles should push all of us into deeper communion with God that will allow us to stand strong against the works of our enemy.

Yes, Gen Z is poised for a fresh outpouring of the Holy Spirit, a new wave of Holy Spirit power that is already sweeping the earth. Yet just being part of this generation does not necessarily mean you will be part of this next great move of the Spirit. No one is going to encounter God for us. If we sit on the sidelines and let someone else pray, worship, and seek the Lord, we will miss this amazing moment in history. Knowing God is an individual experience. "Secondhand spirituality" will not be enough for the challenges of our day. Our father's and grandfather's encounters will simply not suffice. We need our own story, our own encounter for our own time. In my opinion, Gen Z is ready for this kind of personal pursuit of God. I have seen them, spoken with them, heard from them, worshipped with them, and prayed with them, and I can honestly say that Gen Z is hungry for the Holy Spirit. And as Scripture promises, those who are hungry *will* be filled.[118]

ZECHARIAH AND ZERUBBABEL

Zechariah and Zerubbabel are two "Z" people who experienced the Holy Spirit in their generation. They could not live on "secondhand spirituality" because they were in the midst of a drama in which supernatural assistance was needed. The stories of Moses standing before Pharaoh or Joshua at the walls of Jericho were undoubtedly sources of encouragement, yet, past victories were not enough. They needed a contemporary triumph that would help them personally *make* history, not just *remember* it. Ultimately, they would emerge with their own story of God's power.

Our two "Z" men for this chapter lived during the time of King Cyrus, a secular king who, after 70 years of Israelite bondage, fulfilled the prophecy of Jeremiah by allowing the Judean exiles to return to Jerusalem and rebuild the temple. Seven decades earlier, God's judgment on Judah's sin brought disaster at the hands of the Babylonians, who burned the city, tore down the walls, and razed the temple. Zechariah and Zerubbabel were part of a new generation, whose entire lives had been spent in exile. Babylon was their context and living as refugees their experience. A new opportunity was before them to journey to Jerusalem and engage in a restoration project of prophetic proportions. The return to Jerusalem would be fraught with danger and challenge. Zechariah and Zerubbabel traveled with 42,360 exiles in their Jerusalem journey with the unified purpose of restoring worship unto God.[119] Upon arrival, they quickly rebuilt the altar and began work on the temple. Zerubbabel emerged as the construction leader for the project and, ultimately, as the governor of the Jews in Judah and Judea.

The challenges and pressures on Zerubbabel as a leader were severe. When the foundation of the temple was completed, opposition to the work rose from the people living around Jerusalem. The opposition imposed political pressure by writing letters and bribing Syrian officials to slow down the work. When King Cyrus died and his son Cambyses II came to power, these efforts to stop Zerubbabel became successful. To make matters worse, the funding Cyrus promised was redirected to fight Cambyses's war in Egypt.

For more than a decade, construction ceased. The foundation of the temple lay dormant, and the dreams of the people slowly died. However, Ezra recorded, "Now Haggai the prophet and Zechariah the prophet, a descendant of Iddo, prophesied to the Jews in Judah and Jerusalem in the name of the God of Israel, who was over them. Then Zerubbabel son of Shealtiel and Joshua son of Jozadak set to work to rebuild the house of God in Jerusalem. And the prophets of God were with them, supporting them."[120] As Zechariah had prophesied, "This is the word of the LORD to Zerubbabel: 'Not by might nor by power, but by my Spirit,' says the LORD Almighty. 'What are you, mighty mountain? Before Zerubbabel you will become level ground. Then he will bring out the capstone to shouts of "God bless it! God bless it!"'"[121]

Both Haggai and Zechariah prophesied that the building was to continue. It is important to note that nothing appeared to have changed. Zerubbabel heeded the prophecies of Haggai and the "Z" prophet, rallying the people to finish what they had started sixteen years before. Zechariah's promise was that the work would be completed, but *only* by God's Spirit. The pressure and purpose of the moment positioned Zerubbabel and Zechariah to see the Holy Spirit work in their generation.

This was not going to be secondhand spirituality. God was going to reveal Himself as a contemporary to a group of people who had never seen His glory. When the building re-commenced, the opposition also reactivated. Local Syrian officials Tattenai and Shethar-Bozenai wrote a letter to bolster their position, but this time political efforts at stopping the work on the temple backfired. The political winds shifted, or as we could say, the "wind of the Spirit blew."

A new Persian king, Darius, searched the records to find that Cyrus did in fact commission the Jews to rebuild the temple. Because of this, not only did he give the Jews permission to continue building, he ordered the destruction of the homes of anyone who opposed the work. Furthermore, Darius ordered the local officials to provide complete funding and even animals for daily sacrifice in the new temple. What a reversal! Unlikely, improbable, impossible, and yet made possible by the work of God's Spirit. The people finished the temple and restored worship unto God in Jerusalem. And it was not by might, nor by power, but by His Spirit. God's Spirit did what man could not do.

Now, let's reflect on how the Spirit can work in our lives, as seen in the lives of Zerubbabel and Zechariah.

THE HOLY SPIRIT PROVIDES MOTIVATION

The Holy Spirit is like fire. He gives passion, motivation, and spiritual energy. He is the "energy drink of the Spirit," so to speak. When Zechariah and Haggai prophesied by the Holy Spirit, Zerubbabel and the people were motivated in a fresh way to continue with the work despite the opposition.

THE HOLY SPIRIT BREAKS INTIMIDATION

The Spirit gives us courage beyond what is normal. He infuses us with power as God's witnesses, so we know fully that "the one who is in [us] is greater than the one who is in the world."[122] This spirit of courage caused Zerubbabel to continue rebuilding the temple and break free from the intimidation that had halted the people for sixteen years.

THE HOLY SPIRIT OVERCOMES OPPOSITION

The mountain standing in the way of Zerubbabel was a governmental edict, demanding that they discontinue the work on the temple. God had promised him through Zechariah that this mountain would come down, "not by might nor by power, but by [His] Spirit."[123] The decree from the king seemed like an insurmountable obstacle before these two Z leaders in their generation. However, the Holy Spirit is God's mighty mountain mover!

THE HOLY SPIRIT SUPERSEDES LIMITATION

The Holy Spirit gives us immediate, global, personal, and eternal connectivity to the Father. Just as He did with Zerubbabel and those Zerubbabel was leading, the Holy Spirit gives us supernatural empowerment to be and do more than seems possible. He is not limited by our weakness or our greatness. *All* things are possible with Him!

Born for the Spirit

Zerubbabel and Zechariah had to discover the Holy Spirit's power for themselves in their generation. What about us? Will we settle for the stories of the past? Will we live with "secondhand spirituality" our entire lives? Or will we pursue personal encounters and relationships with the Holy Spirit? Will we do more than just study history and instead *make* history? Will we experience the mountain-moving, courage-building, opposition-defeating, supernaturally motivating power of the living God in our generation? Generation Z is born for this moment. Just as Zerubbabel and Zechariah found themselves in a divine drama, even so, this generation is living in a divine drama. God's will must be done, God's house must be built, and the opposition to God's will must be overcome.

The Holy Spirit gives us immediate, global, personal, and eternal connectivity to the Father. Just as He did with Zerubbabel and those Zerubbabel was leading, the Holy Spirit gives us supernatural empowerment to be and do more than seems possible.

The mountains of difficulty that stand in our way are nothing compared to the wind and fire of heaven that go before us. The challenges Generation Z faces are big—*monumental* even—but these mountains will come down as Gen Zers are filled with the Lord's presence and as they obey Him. Facing the mountains is what puts us on our knees and helps open us to the work of the Holy Spirit. Augustine said, "You have made us for yourself, and our hearts are restless until they can find rest in you."[124] The Westminster Catechism states, "Man's chief end is to glorify God, and to enjoy him forever."[125] All of us are born with a God-sized vacuum inside of us, and only when we turn that vacuum toward Jesus, will we fulfill our destiny. From the moment of conception and throughout our lives, God invites us to know Him and to rely on Him when facing the impossible. We were *born* for this!

When I knelt in that Dallas hotel room, facing what I believed were high mountains and feeling very incapable in my own strength, I learned afresh what Generation Z must discover in the challenging days ahead. "God has it, and He has us." God will help us do the impossible by His Spirit. So, if like Zerubbabel and Zechariah—and this aging college president—you are facing the impossible, and you feel as if you are not enough, turn the vacuum of your heart to heaven and hear the word of the Lord:

"This is the word of the LORD to [**insert your name here**]: 'Not by might nor by power, but by my Spirit,' says the LORD Almighty. 'What are you, mighty mountain? Before [**insert your name here**] you will become level ground. Then he will bring out the capstone to shouts of "God bless it! God bless it!""[126]

CHAPTER FIVE

A GENERATION BORN FOR HOPE: ZEPHANIAH

It ranks as one of the worst days of my life. The call came on a summer evening just after work. It was the kind of call a university president never wants to receive. A tragedy had taken place. Darkness fell over my heart in waves as the news came through the phone that one of our lady athletes was found dead in her dorm room. And the deepest pain of all was that the cause appeared to be suicide, an epidemic I later learned had increased 56 percent among young people ages ten to twenty-four, from 2007 to 2017.[127] The emotions of that moment were beyond any I have experienced as president. Grief, sadness, anger, disappointment, and a sense of failure flooded my heart while a host of accompanying questions like "Why?" "What?" "How?" "When?" and "Where?" washed through my mind.

I rushed to the dorm room where I found her wingmates, coaches, and fellow athletes in tearful shock. We stood weeping together with many more questions than answers. As time passed, we learned that in a moment of despair (perhaps due to romantic disappointment), this beautiful young lady with an amazingly bright future decided to make the ultimate decision of attempting to take her own life. We discovered that she may have been trying to send out a cry of despair more than a desire for death. Yet, the resulting finality brought darkness to her family, friends, teammates, and community that was devastating. Tough, gut-wrenching hours and days ensued. The team survived, and her sister even played her final year with stellar results, but combating the darkness and finding hope amid the despair was not easy.

More obvious to me every day is the fact that the greatest need in our world and in this generation is hope. The leader of the Reformation, Martin Luther, once said, "Everything that is done in the world is done by hope."[128] Hal Lindsey, American evangelist and Christian writer, has been quoted as saying, "Man can live about forty days without food, about three days without water, about eight minutes without air... but only for one second without hope."[129]

Hope is necessary for human life. Where it is lacking, darkness and death prevail. Unfortunately, a hope-filled world is not the kind Gen Z has been born into. Instead, today's youth have been handed a world filled with darkness, death, and despair. Their struggle to find optimism and courage is significant and real. As I continually have stated throughout this book, I believe this *now* generation of men and women is indeed the greatest in the history of the world, which is why I also believe they are a generation under immense spiritual attacks. At times, these attacks are not only against their spiritual health but also against their physical, emotional, and mental health.

Martin Luther, once said, "Everything that is done in the world is done by hope."

The National Institute of Mental Health reported that in 2017, "an estimated 3.2 million adolescents aged 12 to 17 in the United States had at least one major depressive episode. This number represented 13.3% of the US population aged 12 to 17."[130] In 2020, the World Health Organization stated that "Depression is a leading cause of disability worldwide and a major contributor to the overall global burden of disease. Globally, more than 264 million people of all ages suffer from depression."[131] Health insurer Cigna recently reported that loneliness and the perception of being lonely were identified at epidemic proportions, especially among young adults ages eighteen to twenty-two in the US. They claim, "Generation Z (adults ages 18–22) is the loneliest generation and claims to be in worse health than older generations."[132] OneHope recently released their *Global Youth Culture U.S. Report*, which gives insight into various tendencies and struggles that influence digitally connected teens in the US. The report shares that within a three-month period, 74 percent of teens admit feeling loneliness, 66 percent say they have felt high anxiety, and 60 percent have experienced depression.[133]

Youth suicide has exploded in the twenty-first century. It is now the second-leading cause of death around the world for those ages fifteen to twenty-four, and according to the Centers for Disease Control and Prevention (CDC), suicidal thoughts, planning, and attempts are significantly higher among adults ages eighteen to twenty-nine than they are among adults thirty and older.[134] From 1999 to 2017, the age-adjusted suicide rate increased 33 percent,[135] causing the National Institute of Mental Health to call suicide "a major public health concern" with "twice as many suicides (47,173) in the United States as there were homicides (19,510)" in 2017.[136] *Global Youth Culture U.S. Report* shares that 35 percent of teens in the US reported having had suicidal thoughts within a three-month period, making it the highest rate of any country in their global study. Seven percent said they actually attempted to take their own life.[137]

Depression, self-harm, and suicide stem from various sources of stress. The American Psychological Association

(APA) said that "61% of college students seeking counseling report anxiety, 49% report depression, 45% report stress, 31% report family issues, 28% report stress from academic performance and 27% report stress from relationship problems."[138]

Now, that is *a lot* of stress. This infiltration of despair has taken a nosedive in recent years as shown by the APA, which reported that Gen Z is "significantly more likely (27 percent) than other generations . . . to report their mental health as fair or poor . . . They are also more likely (37 percent) . . . to report they have received treatment or therapy from a mental health professional. . . ."[139] The need for counseling on college campuses has exploded, and Christian universities are not exempt. In a recent meeting with independent and predominantly Christian university presidents, one of the top needs identified across our campuses was student mental health. At ORU, we have opened a new, free student counseling center with licensed counselors prepared to help students walk through life's toughest situations.

All of these statistics affirm my own observations. Gen Z deals with loneliness, fear, paranoia, and, many times, morbidity at an unprecedented level. They have expressed their anguish, lack of understanding of their identity, and depression in many ways; some of the worst include self-harm and suicide. My questions are "Why is this happening?" and "Why is such an anointed, talented, potential-filled generation facing such a mountain of emotional and mental turmoil?" In a simple answer: the enemy—the prince of darkness—knows who they are and what they are capable of, and he is trying desperately to stop them.

If you look closely, you will discover that Satan's tactics are subtle and targeted. In a world that is bigger than it has ever been, numbering more than 7.8 billion people,[140] he primarily attacks young people's sense of significance and their need for community. When we consider that 60 percent of Gen Zers report a strong desire to want to change the world, as compared to 39 percent of the generation before them,[141] it is clear how they can easily feel hopeless to make their mark in such a huge world. We also know that God has designed humankind for community. In a world as enormous as ours, Gen Z often turns to the use of technology—apps, social media sites, and messaging—to connect with people around the world, spending more than 11 hours per day in digital engagement.[142] But as many reports have shown, this attempt at connectivity and community can easily backfire and often does.

Gen Z deals with loneliness, fear, paranoia, and, many times, morbidity at an unprecedented level.

Social psychologist Jean M. Twenge stated in an article for *The Atlantic* magazine that spending more time on social media and other screen activities correlates strongly with lower levels of happiness and higher feelings of loneliness, levels of depression, and risk of suicide.[143] Columnist Stephen Marche said, "An ironic negative effect of digital technology on teenagers and on humanity is that of isolation. Even though in today's world we are more connected than ever before in history with our 'digital global village,' humans are lonelier and suffer from more depression than ever before in history."[144] Gen Zers long for *genuine* relationships, yet they are seeking them through *counterfeit* means. This leaves them connected yet isolated, savvy but anxious, blessed, definitely, but also stressed.

Besides these external stressors, internal pressures also seem to plague Gen Z just as they have generations before them. One of the most significant of these is their past wounds still unhealed. Unreconciled issues wedge themselves deeply into the heart and soul of an individual, causing them to struggle to have a positive outlook on the world. Abuse is a major contributor. *The Huffington Post* published an article stating: "Every 98 seconds someone in the U.S.A. is sexually assaulted."[145] This means mean that 881.6 people experience sexual violence in our country every single day. The CDC states that "1 in 5 women and 1 out of every 71 men will be raped at some point in their lives."[146] A report from Darkness to Light, a child abuse prevention organization, states, "1 out of every 10 children will be sexually abused by their 18th birthday."[147]

In addition to abuse, premarital sex has also deeply wounded this generation. Although it is a wound of their own design, it is a wound, nonetheless. The CDC says that "youth ages 15 to 24 make up just over one quarter of the sexually active population" and "account for half of the 20 million new sexually transmitted infections that occur in the United States each year."[148] Personal trauma added to a struggle with sexual sin causes great conflict within the human soul. This inner turmoil fills hearts with a lack of hope and leads to some of the terrible effects we have discussed.

A cursory reading of the New Testament—even just a simple reading of the book of John—will tell you immediately that the world Jesus came into was very much the same. Our hopelessness was His call to enter the world of darkness and bring light. Throughout His ministry, Jesus searched desperate places and forlorn people. He visited places like the Pool of Bethesda and ministered to the dying. He touched the lepers, healed the blind, delivered the demon-possessed, cared for the wounded, blessed the cursed, brought clarity to the relationally dysfunctional, and comforted the psychologically distressed.

Even when dying on the cross, Jesus focused on bringing hope to the hopeless. One of the men hanging next to Him had spent his life in criminal activity and was enduring execution for his crimes. Despite His agonizing pain, Jesus brought him hope, promising they would soon be together in paradise. Jesus consistently reached out to people who were in the deepest despondency. His message of hope penetrated to the core of human anguish, bringing light into prisons of emotional and spiritual darkness. The best part is that He continues to do the same today.

Jesus specifically targeted the next generation with hope, especially in the face of death. He raised several people to life in the New Testament, and of those recorded in the gospels, all were young—Lazarus, Jairus' daughter, and the son of a widow from Nain. Over and over again, He entered into the morbidity and darkness surrounding young generations to bring hope and life amid death. Ultimately, Jesus demonstrated victory over death through His resurrection, and it was this resurrection that brought the explosion of hope our world was desperately searching for. Because of Jesus' example, I agree with Clare Boothe Luce, the author and politician who said, "There really is no hopeless situation. There are only people who have grown hopeless about them."[149]

Gen Z can find hope amid the despair surrounding their generation. The statistics around mental health, depression, and death are significant (just reading the statistics on depression is depressing), yet God gives us a message of hope even when darkness is closing in. God has a *good* plan for us, one that is *always* filled with love, hope, and mercy. As Gen Z trusts this good plan, they will bring a unique perspective to their generation. They will become hope-givers, even in situations that seem the most hopeless. Our "Z" person from Scripture for this chapter did just that.

ZEPHANIAH

Zephaniah was a contemporary of the prophet Jeremiah. Both prophesied to Judah at a time of impending judgment and its accompanying despair. For those who have read the brief, minor prophet book written by Zephaniah, you may be wondering why I would pick this "Z" man as a person to demonstrate hope. After all, Zephaniah's prophecies are some of the most scathing in all of Scripture. If Jeremiah was the weeping prophet, Zephaniah was a prophet on fire. The book of Zephaniah is one of the most judgment-oriented books in history, let alone in Scripture. Zephaniah's first prophetic declaration is: "'I will sweep away everything from the face of the earth,' declares the Lord."[150] In his book, Zephaniah declares God's judgment on the nations of the earth and the peoples surrounding Jerusalem. Most importantly, he joins Jeremiah in proclaiming judgment against Jerusalem and

Judah for their pride and lack of repentance, declaring: "I will stretch out my hand against Judah and against all who live in Jerusalem."[151] Yet during the dark days of judgment and despite the despair of the times, Zephaniah weaves into his book a message of hope.

Throughout his writing, Zephaniah consistently focuses on the fact that God is merciful. In Zephaniah's day, Jerusalem and Judah deserved great punishment, and according to what he had heard from God, chastisement was on its way. Zephaniah and Jeremiah both prophesied to God's people that Babylon would come from the north and take over the city of Jerusalem, bringing judgment on them because of their sin. Yet, Zephaniah promised that even in their despair, God would reveal His mercy and love them through it all.

In Zephaniah 2:3, he said, "Seek the LORD, all you humble of the land, you who do what he commands. Seek righteousness, seek humility; perhaps you will be sheltered on the day of the Lord's anger." Later he encouraged them:

Sing, Daughter Zion;
shout aloud, Israel!
Be glad and rejoice with all your heart,
Daughter Jerusalem!
The LORD has taken away your punishment,
he has turned back your enemy.
The LORD, the King of Israel, is with you;
never again will you fear any harm.
On that day they will say to Jerusalem,
"Do not fear, Zion; do not let your hands hang limp.
The LORD your God is with you,

the Mighty Warrior who saves.
He will take great delight in you;
in his love he will no longer rebuke you,
but will rejoice over you with singing."[152]

Amazing! From the message of God wiping them out to
His singing over them, God's mercy and hope would make
the difference. What a beautiful picture for this generation.
In desolation, God still wants to rejoice over us with singing.
God's mercy endures *forever*. It is everlasting—new every
morning. Mercy can be defined as "not getting what you
deserve," as opposed to grace, which is "getting what you do
not deserve." God's glory is to show mercy.

We often assume judgment and mercy are opposites, but
that is not true. God's judgment on our sin is really His mercy
at work, saving us from greater pain in the future. He sees our
need for correction, and He tells us in His Word that we *know*
we are His children because of how He corrects us.[153] He will
judge our sins and help us adjust our course because of His
great mercy. Even God's judgment on Judah and Jerusalem
was for correction—not destruction—though it felt horrific.
For *all* who are His sons and daughters, God's momentary
discipline is necessary for long-term, hope-filled results. His
intent is always to bring forth *good*.

We see this truth reflected in John's narrative account
of an adulterous woman. She was about to be stoned after
getting caught in the act of adultery. Overtaken by sexual
passion, her secret affair had been discovered. By God's law,
she was to die. (The man was also supposed to die though
I am not sure where he was.)[154] Yet, Jesus extended to her

the Father's mercy. She would not get what she deserved. The religious leaders sought to back Jesus into a corner by asking Him if they should follow the law's command to stone her. His reply was simple yet profound. "Let he who is without sin cast the first stone."[155] At this, every person laid down their cold, blunt instruments of execution and walked away.

Jesus asked the woman, "Has no one condemned you?" Her reply was, "No one, sir." And He communicated both mercy and judgment by saying, "Then neither do I condemn you...go now and leave your life of sin."[156]

In other words, when God sees us bruised, about to break or burn out, He will not break us nor extinguish our flame.

This defining moment in this woman's life gave her both course correction and mercy. This is exactly how God works with all of His children. He is merciful enough to correct us so that we do not run off a cliff, so to speak, and destroy our lives. But He does so in a way that will not torture us. Instead, He desires to *save* us. I love the passage in which Matthew repeats the Lord's words spoken centuries earlier through Isaiah: "A bruised reed he will not break, and a smoldering wick he will not snuff out, till he has brought justice through to victory. In his name the nations will put their hope."[157] In other words, when God sees us bruised, about to break or burn out, He will not break us nor extinguish our flame. Instead, He will lovingly work with us to nurture us, heal us, and bring us back to life until the fire is burning again.

Without a doubt, Gen Zers, like all of us, will feel hopeless at times. That is when we must know that what seems like intense judgment is really God's mercy at work. It is meant to restore us—not to destroy us. As the psalmist assures us, "put your hope in the LORD, for with the LORD is unfailing love and with him is full redemption."[158]

God Is Not Finished Yet

When Zephaniah prophesied to God's people, he made it clear to them that though it may have felt as if their lives were over, God was not through with them yet. Even the weeping prophet Jeremiah encouraged himself with these words: "'The LORD is my portion; therefore I will wait for him.' The LORD is good to those whose hope is in him, to the one who seeks him."[159] In the same way, when we embrace God's judgment instead of avoiding it, we can find hope during hard times, knowing fully that He is not finished with us yet.

One reason we often struggle with despair is that we calculate our lives incorrectly. We add up the total before God has finished working. We assume defeat before the timer hits zero. This brings unnecessary despair and causes us to want to check out. You may very well be in a tough spot right now. Things may feel extremely difficult. You may think there is no way out of or through the problem. Satan is lying to you. God loves you! He is merciful, and He is *not* finished with you yet. He *will* show you a way through the darkest of times if you will allow Him to. He has *good* things in store for you. As long as you have breath, you can have hope that God is still at work in your life on the earth. When encouraging those facing trials and temptations to be patient, James recalled Job and wrote,

"As you know, we count as blessed those who have persevered. You have heard of Job's perseverance and have seen what the Lord finally brought about. The Lord is full of compassion and mercy."[160]

God Always Has a Plan

The final lesson we can learn from Zephaniah's message of hope is not only that God is merciful and has not given up on us, but also that He always has a plan. Perhaps one of the best-known and most inspiring verses in the Bible came from our "Z" prophet's contemporary, Jeremiah, who was talking to the same people—declaring the same impending doom that Zephaniah was—when he prophesied, "'For I know the plans I have for you,' declares the LORD, 'plans to prosper you and not to harm you, plans to give you hope and a future'"[161]

During these days when many Gen Zers are struggling with depression, self-harm, and a loss of hope, we must remind them that God *still* has a plan. He wants to meet us where we are and lift us into the light and life He brings.

Hope Over Hurt

In October 1856, a popular twenty-two-year-old preacher named Charles Spurgeon prepared to speak in a secular arena. For the first time, the grand Surrey Music Hall in London would be used for gospel declaration. Reporters, writers, and religious leaders throughout England were aghast that he would preach in a secular arena, so they filled the communication avenues of the day with their criticism of young Spurgeon. Did he not understand that places of secular entertainment should not be used for sacred purposes? Nevertheless,

Spurgeon ignored his critics, planning a large crusade in the beautiful music hall.

On opening night, twelve thousand people squished together inside the building with ten thousand more listening from outside. Just as Spurgeon stepped into the pulpit to deliver God's Word to the excited crowd, someone yelled, "Fire! Fire! The galleries are giving way!" Suddenly, pandemonium broke loose in the jam-packed arena as people rushed toward the exits to escape the purported fire. (It was later discovered that this was just a prank; there was no fire at all.) Spurgeon stood in shock on the stage as the tragedy unfolded. Several were trampled while those in the crowd tried to exit and those waiting outside tried to enter. Within moments, seven people lay dead and twenty-eight others were severely injured. Spurgeon tried to continue his message but to no avail. As the extent of the disaster grew clearer, he was overcome with both grief and guilt. He supposed that perhaps the critics were right. Perhaps he never should have tried using a secular arena to preach the gospel. Several men carried Spurgeon to his carriage as he retreated from the Surrey Music Hall horror scene.[162]

This was the darkest moment of Spurgeon's young life. He was taken to a house nearby and for two weeks, he fought with depression, despair, and hopelessness. He later said he was "in tears by day, and dreams of terror by night."[163] The press and his critics (including fellow preachers) attacked him incessantly. The famous young preacher's ministry appeared to be over, and the darkness surrounding him seemed impenetrable. Spurgeon later said of this time that "There are dungeons beneath the Castle of Despair as dreary as the abodes of the lost, and some of us have been in them."[164]

During those two weeks, Spurgeon spent much time outside, walking in the garden and pouring his heart out to God. Somewhere amid his despair, God's light broke through and new courage replaced the depression. Within weeks, Spurgeon returned to Surrey Music Hall, and for the next three years, he preached a message of hope from that grand hall, resulting in thousands of people converting to Christianity. The place of disaster and despondency became a place of delight for Spurgeon. God's mercy brought great hope out of deep despair.[165]

God did the same for me following that precious, potential-filled student's death. He brought hope in the midst of darkness, igniting in me an even deeper passion than I had before to convince Generation Z of the unfailing hope found in Jesus Christ. As I walked out of the dorm that difficult night, I felt overwhelming anger at the prince of darkness. The audacity he had to convince a member of the great Generation Z that life was hopeless made my blood boil! I want Satan and his kingdom to pay for convincing that young woman that her life was not worth living. I want to impact Generation Z in such a way that hope will fill their hearts and they will never count things finished before God's work is finished in them. I want them to never give up in judgment, but to hold on until they see God's mercy break through. I want them to cling to hope despite all odds, believing God's promise that He has a good plan for their lives. And when they grab onto this hope, I am confident that they, too, will punish the prince of darkness by spreading the light of our King.

Jesus is alive, and He came to bring life to this generation. Just as He sought young men and women to raise from the dead, even so, the living Jesus of the twenty-first century will visit the spiritual tombs of a generation with the power of resurrection in His voice. He has won the victory for them. Hope has been secured. Death has been defeated. Despair has been dispersed and depression has been turned into delight by our Savior. Generation Z can overcome demonic mental, emotional, and physical attacks against them. They were born for hope. Hope's name is *Jesus*!

CHAPTER SIX
A GENERATION BORN FOR INTEGRITY: ZACCHAEUS

"**D**o you solemnly swear to tell the truth, the whole truth and nothing but the truth, so help you, God?" The correct answer is "I do." I heard this phrase regularly during my early childhood days. No, I was not raised in a courtroom—far from it, actually. But I did watch television after school, and at our house, we always tuned in to the *Perry Mason* show (ancient history for Gen Zers, but you can Google it). Over and over again, Mr. Mason called witnesses to the stand, and they committed themselves to this legal oath. The oath, or some version of it in affirmation form, is still used in courtrooms across America and around the world to ensure that witnesses understand the gravity of their testimony and the potential of being charged with perjury.

The origin of both this statement and practice probably comes from thirteenth-century England. It has continued through the years and was carried over into the courtrooms of America, thus finding its way onto the *Perry Mason* show. However, the history of some form of commitment to truth-telling as part of legal proceedings dates back to ancient times. One reason for the oath may have been captured by the early Greek Christian scholar Origen when he stated: "Conscience is the chamber of justice."[166] The witness oath, then, is used in legally binding situations to awaken the conscience, many times toward God and in the fear of God. Back then, the oath ended, as it still does in some courtrooms, with "so help me God," helping the witness to remember that God is listening and recording the testimony, not just the court clerk. According to a decision by the Missouri Supreme Court in 1890, the purpose of an oath as a feature of a legal proceeding is its "'quickening of the conscience.' State v. Bennet, 14 S.W. 865 (Mo. 1890)."[167]

Although as a young boy I heard people take this oath every week on *Perry Mason*, I never really contemplated what telling the truth—"the whole truth and nothing but the truth"— meant. In fact, it has only been within the last several years—after encountering hundreds of people with hundreds of stories—that I have realized how very possible it is to not tell a lie while also not telling "the whole truth and nothing but the truth." Sadly, the newer generations are skilled at this. Subtle deception, white lies, and the capacity to share less than the whole truth, these are words and actions that swirl around us every day. It seems to me that our generation is due for a new "quickening of the conscience."

Generation Z specifically has grown up in a world filled with deception and moral compromise, and their estimation of truth has been affected. In a recent Barna study on Gen Z regarding their attitudes on moral issues, it was confirmed that this generation's embrace of moral absolutes continues to deteriorate. Truth-telling, or the lack thereof, was one of the key issues in the study that revealed a significant decline. Elders (the Greatest Generation) are a shrinking proportion of the overall population, but for perspective, fully three out of five among the eldest generation (61 percent) strongly agreed in the Barna survey that lying was immoral, while only approximately one out of three (33.3 percent) in Gen Z believed lying was wrong. Even among baby boomers, more than 50 percent still believed lying was evil according to Barna, though many of them do not always live what they believe.[168] Since God's Word states that *"all* liars. . . will be consigned to the lake of fire,"[169] it is little wonder that Isaiah declared: "hell hath enlarged herself, and opened her mouth without measure."[170]

Truth-telling is key to living a life of integrity, and integrity is key to Generation Z's ability to lead in the future. Secular and spiritual leaders throughout history have understood the power of integrity and its connection to truth-telling. Solomon, in his wisdom, stated: "The LORD detests lying lips, but he delights in people who are trustworthy."[171] General Dwight D. Eisenhower said: "The supreme quality for leadership is unquestionably integrity. Without it, no real success is possible, no matter whether it is on a section gang, a football field, in an army, or in an office."[172] Henry Kravis stated: "If you don't have integrity, you have nothing. You can't buy it. You can have all the money in the world, but if you are not a moral and ethical person, you really have nothing."[173] Zig Ziglar declared, "Honesty and integrity are absolutely essential for success in life—all areas of life. The really good news is that anyone can develop both honesty and integrity."[174] Our ministry friend Joyce Meyer reminds us that "integrity means you are the same in private as you are in public."[175] And finally, even Ralph Waldo Emerson, who was not a spiritual leader to be emulated, stated, "I cannot find language of sufficient energy to convey my sense of the sacredness of private integrity."[176]

Truth-telling is key to living a life of integrity, and integrity is key to Generation Z's ability to lead in the future.

"Integrity" is derived from the root word "integer," which means "whole" or "a complete entity,"[177] the opposite of "fractional" or "divided." Integrity is soundness, dependability, trustworthiness, and wholeness. Integrity is not just about telling the truth in court or the public square. It is about telling the truth to yourself and to God. Integrity will be critical for Gen Z as they bear the pressure of leadership in the twenty-first century, and—in my opinion—it is one of the greatest issues they must conquer.

The Defeat of Duplicity

Proverbs 11:3 says, "The integrity of the upright guides them, but the unfaithful are destroyed by their duplicity." The apostle James said, "A double minded man is unstable in all his ways."[178] Double-mindedness, or "spiritual duplicity," parades itself daily in the marketplace and church-place alike. The segmentation of one's life is now embraced across the cultures of the world. People have a spiritual life, a secular life, a romantic life, a work life, a family life, a private life, a social media life—and the list could go on. Many times, these segmented portions of existence are approached differently and embraced with different value systems, all from the same person. In other words, people may live like a heavenly angel in church on Sunday and act like a fallen angel at work on Monday. Amazingly, the numbed conscience of a generation, branded by the lusts of the flesh is rarely awakened to what this duplicity is doing to them or the destruction it foretells.

Through the years, I have encountered spiritual duplicity in numerous counseling sessions during which individuals who have committed gross sins deny that they really did what the evidence proved true. At other times, they have said to me something like, "Yes, I did do that, but that is not how I felt in my heart. That action was not really me." Students and others have described the emotions they felt when failing spiritually and said it was as if they were watching themselves on a screen, all the while claiming that their heart remained good while their flesh acted badly. These lives are fractured—as all of ours have been at one time—and are not integrous. Fractured, dissonant lives *must* be made whole, or destruction awaits.

Though man has always struggled with duplicity, this problem seems especially acute in this generation. Every year, I am amazed at a small subset of students who, when they arrive at our university, simply do not seem capable of telling the truth. Some of them do not endure the culture at ORU, while many others are changed, thank God, so we are patient with them. From false excuses regarding their absence from class and false claims of prior accomplishments to subtle deceptions attempting to avoid the repercussions truth might bring them, these habitual deceivers represent people in our culture that seem to be on the run, living multiple lives and feeling spiritually schizophrenic. We might do well to remember Mark Twain's comforting-yet-challenging statement: "If you tell the truth, you don't have to remember anything."[179]

Fractured, dissonant lives *must* be made whole, or destruction awaits.

We watch this struggle for truth every day by tuning into national media, as politicians and others seek to manipulate their message in a way most beneficial to them or their party. The "spin" goes out of control, leaving the entire world wondering what exactly is true in a given situation. At times, I feel like rising with the prophet Isaiah to declare that "truth is fallen in the street."[180]

Added to this struggle for truth are the doctrines of license that have swept through the global church. I was raised "Pentecostal strict." Laughingly, we used to claim that we did not "drink, smoke, or chew or run with people that do." Many times, the church I grew up in was more concerned with the letter of the law than with the spirit of the law. Holiness deteriorated into lists, and hypocrisy was the result. We seemed to work diligently to keep the negatives of the faith while at times neglecting the positives of it. Over several years of my ministry, I spoke, preached, and worked against the hard coldness of legalistic Christianity. Our hope was for a spiritual breakthrough that would allow new generations to live in greater spiritual freedom in an authentic, loving relationship with Jesus instead of a fabricated religious experience. While my lifestyle remained conservative, for which I am very grateful, my perspective broadened to love those who needed it the most—including the legalists. Through it all, I learned that legalism is a cruel taskmaster and kills spiritual vitality. Yet, in my lifetime, I have watched the pendulum swing in the Spirit-empowered movement from legalism with its accompanying hypocrisy to licentiousness with its accompanying reproach.

Millions of Christians around the world have thrown off constraint. Drunkenness, adultery, same-sex relationships, stealing, lying, vindictiveness, jealousy, hatred, fleshly indulgence, filthy language—and the list goes on—have all been accepted as "just how things are" in Christian ranks. In the midst of this, an ancient lie has resurfaced that tells us our hearts can remain pure even when our bodies commit impure deeds. This philosophy is not new. Paul battled this in the early church where he taught against both legalism and license. On one hand, Paul combated the Judaizers who were demanding outward conformity to religious practice from the converted Gentiles. Paul preached a message of freedom in Christ and freedom from the chains of empty religious practice. On the other hand, Paul also fought against licentiousness and numerous philosophies that subtly justified sin, including the influence of Gnosticism.

Gnosticism, which Paul consistently spoke against in his writings, was a doctrine that infiltrated early Christianity. The Greek word *gnosis* means "knowledge." In the Gnostic's belief, this special knowledge was necessary for salvation. The Merriam-Webster Dictionary defines *gnosis* as "esoteric knowledge of spiritual truth held by the ancient Gnostics to be essential to salvation."[181] Ultimately, this pursuit of special knowledge led to a division of the material world from the spiritual world. For the individual, this translated into a separation of the spiritual man from the physical man. Table 6.1 below provides some of the differences between Gnosticism and true Christianity. Some early Christian communities blended the two. Gnostic teaching led to the understanding that since the material body was formed, the flesh was inherently evil, and the spirit was inherently good. If you had this special knowledge, then you were counted "saved" no matter what you did with your material or physical self. In other words, the separation of spirit and flesh allowed you to do whatever you wanted with your flesh (because it was evil anyway) as long as your spirit remained pure and filled with the knowledge of who you really were.

	CHRISTIAN VIEW	GNOSTIC VIEW
God	One, triune God who wants to be known.	Two opposing gods: 1) Supreme; Unknown; Distant 2) Demiurge – Evil Creator
World	Initially created by God and declared "good" by Him and is currently under the curse due to humanity's sin.	Material world (matter) is inherently Evil.
Christ	100% divine, 100% human incarnational presence of the Holy Spirit. Died on the cross for our sins.	Spiritual, divine being that looked like a human being. Did not suffer on the cross. Denied the humanity of Christ.
Salvation	Only by the belief in the death, burial, and resurrection of Jesus for our sins.	Only the "enlightened" ones, who received the secret "saving" knowledge, could be freed from "evil" matter.

Table 6.1: Differences between Christian and Gnostic viewpoints[182]

Fast forward to the twenty-first century, and modern quasi-Gnostic teaching might sound something like this: "You must know that you are the righteousness of God in Christ. As long as you know this, you are victorious. Your physical actions are not important as long as you know who you are. All of your sins — past, present, and future — were taken care of by Christ's righteousness, so you should never think about them again. Just *know* that you are righteous, and you *are.*" It is alarming how many believe this false teaching.

Ultimately, the old lie that your physical actions do not matter as long as your spirit remains pure and your identity in Christ stays strong leads to the moral deterioration we see in many "Christian" circles. Now as then, these teachings are *close* to the truth, which makes them difficult to discern and defeat. We *do* need to know who we are in Christ, and we *do* need to trust fully in His righteousness and not our own works. But what we do with our bodies *does* matter! The tendency to separate physical action from spiritual condition leads to a generation that cannot own their sins as well as to individuals who believe their hearts have remained right while their bodies have committed gross immorality. In all spiritual gentleness, I want to state clearly that this doctrine is a *lie!*

> The tendency to separate physical action from spiritual condition leads to a generation that cannot own their sins as well as to individuals who believe their hearts have remained right while their bodies have committed gross immorality.

The Bible teaches that our love for and relationship with God must lead to obedience if it is to be acceptable. Jesus clearly said, "If you love me, keep my commands."[183] John later confirmed, "If we claim to have fellowship with him and yet walk in the darkness, we lie and do not live out the truth … We know that we have come to know him if we keep his commands. Whoever says, 'I know him,' but does not do what he commands is a liar, and the truth is not in that person."[184]

Paul consistently confronted these trends toward duplicity and Gnosticism by listing things that were sinful, encouraging victory over the flesh, and helping believers own their sins. In his theology, the cross became the centerpiece — the only hope for bringing unity and wholeness to man. In the cross, we see both the dreadfulness of our sins and the powerfulness of Christ's salvation. Jesus fully engaged the evil of the world as 100 percent man while breaking its power over us as 100 percent God. The cross brought the spiritual and material worlds together in God's redemptive work. By the cross, we can repent and be freed from those things that divide our lives before God. In Jesus and because of the cross, our spirits, minds (souls), and bodies can be united in total consecration.

> Our duty is to teach young men and women to own their failures before God, confess their sins, trust in His forgiveness, and then enjoy the inner peace of integrity.

The idea that our hearts can remain pure while our bodies sin *must* be confronted in this generation. Our duty is to teach young men and women to own their failures before God, confess their sins, trust in His forgiveness, and then enjoy the inner peace of integrity. Integrity happens when the actions of our bodies agree with the intent of our hearts and souls. Integrity is when we love God with our complete being, including our strength. Integrity (or being whole) means that the false divisions between who we say we are and how we live are resolved, allowing our lives to be unified. To the Thessalonians, who were encountering the teachings of the Gnostics, Paul said, "May God himself, the God of peace, sanctify you through and through. May your whole spirit, soul and body be kept blameless at the coming of our Lord Jesus Christ."[185] Our decision to follow Jesus initiates a radical transformation in our lives. Things can never and *must* never be the same again. Our divided lives must become unified before Him.

ZACCHAEUS

Winston Churchill, Napoleon Bonaparte, Mahatma Gandhi, Charlie Chaplin, J. R. R. Tolkien, Robert Downey Jr., Prince, and Tom Cruise became famous for different reasons, yet they share one similarity: their height of smaller than five feet, eight inches. Hundreds of vertically challenged men and women have made history and affected the record books. Height is not a prerequisite for greatness as Israel discovered with King Saul, who was a head taller than all others. Added to the list of famous short men in the world is our "Z" man for this chapter — Zacchaeus.

All we know of Zacchaeus is located in just one chapter of the Bible: Luke 19. Our star for the moment was the chief tax collector of his region. He worked as an emissary of the state in one of the toughest, most cursed places on earth: Jericho.

Zacchaeus was rich. He had overachieved within his dusty district, and though he had plenty of money, he lacked integrity. His reputation preceded him wherever he went, and it was not good.

Maria Razumich-Zec, an executive with The Peninsula Hotels group, one of the most trusted brands in the hotel industry, has said, "Your reputation and integrity are everything. Follow through on what you say you're going to do. Your credibility can only be built over time, and it is built from the history of your words and actions."[186] Well, Zacchaeus built his reputation over time, and the word that those who knew him best used to describe him was not a positive one. It was "sinner." After a while, Zacchaeus's wealth and accomplishments left him empty. He knew he was missing something. As Scripture tells us, that "something" actually turned out to be "Some*one*."

Jesus arrived in Jericho at the height of His ministry and healed blind Bartimaeus on His way into town. As word of this dramatic miracle flashed like wildfire across the community, hundreds of Jericho villagers crowded around Jesus. Zacchaeus was curious, too. He wanted to meet the Healer. He wanted to connect with this man whose reputation for doing good preceded Him.

Because of Zacchaeus's physical stature, he could not see over the crowd, so he ran ahead of Jesus' entourage and climbed up in a sycamore tree for a better view. There he was—a wealthy sinner—out on a limb and risking it all for just one glimpse of glory. When Jesus arrived where Zacchaeus was, He stopped and called for him to come down out of the tree. Jesus then invited Himself to the home of the tax collector, which quickly set off a flurry of gossip. Luke records that Zacchaeus welcomed Jesus gladly. He went from straining to catch just a glimpse of glory to hosting Him at his home. It was quite a dramatic and significant change for Zacchaeus. The people could not believe that Jesus, the Healer of the blind, would go to the house of this sinner.

As Zacchaeus climbed down the tree after hearing Jesus declare, "I'm going home with you!" something transitioned. Zacchaeus was converted by the focused attention and love of Jesus. He welcomed Jesus gladly, not only to his physical house but also into his empty heart. Zacchaeus, ever the over-achiever, immediately began the journey to integrity resto-ration. He declared, "Look, Lord! Here and now I give half of my possessions to the poor, and if I have cheated anybody out of anything, I will pay back four times the amount."[187]

Zacchaeus's heart was changed, so his actions changed as well. He went from being the tax collector exacting payments (and perhaps *over*payments) from the residents of Jericho to becoming their biggest benefactor—all in one day, or actually, all in one *moment*! Meeting Jesus put Zacchaeus on the road to integrity where his flesh and bank account would now agree with his heart. Jesus declared, "Today salvation has come to this house, because this man, too, is a son of Abraham. For the Son of Man came to seek and to save the lost."[188] Zacchaeus's desire to make things right was a true sign of salvation.

Integrity Restored

Early in my ministry, I was speaking at a church in a college town where my best childhood friend was living with his girl-friend. This friend was close to me growing up, and we did everything together. He was in my wedding, but I had not seen him in a couple of years by that time. I remember the feeling I had when the Lord impressed upon me strongly that I needed to go see him and his girlfriend while I was in town. You see, the girl he was living with—who would ultimately become his wife—was someone I had dated before I was fully following Jesus. I had been less than a gentleman with her, and now the Lord was pressing me to go apologize for my misbehavior. Reluctantly, I gathered the courage to obey, though I did stall as long as I could. The butterflies in my stomach almost choked me as I approached the door to their apartment on my last morning in town.

Maybe they won't be home, and I'll be off the hook, I thought. I knocked on the door, waited a few moments, and started to flee just as the girl opened the door. Her boyfriend, my childhood best friend, was not home. It was a very unusual moment. I stood outside the door as I shared with her my testimony about how my life had radically changed and that I was now following Jesus fully. I also shared why I felt the need to visit with her and apologize. Expressing sorrow for my actions, I asked her to forgive me. She listened and responded graciously. As I left the door of the apartment, my heart was free. I had obeyed the Spirit and, more importantly, had closed a door to the past. That night, I preached with a new, fresh anointing as well as greatly increased results.

Several years later, I received a call that this same childhood best friend had been killed in a tragic private airplane crash, leaving his wife—the girl to whom I had apologized— and two children behind. The funeral was large, with many friends and family filling the church. After the service, I stepped forward to shake hands with my friend's wife and express my condolences. I looked her square in the eye and told her that my wife and I were sorry this had happened. I assured her that I would be praying for her. It was an amazing moment to realize there was nothing between us. No soul tie or attraction existed whatsoever. My awkward visit to her college town apartment several years before had closed the door to the past and had allowed me to walk into that funeral with integrity.

The Holy Spirit working in Zacchaeus's heart communicated to him that to live with integrity and wholeness, he needed to repair any pain his broken life had caused.

This story is proof that lost integrity can be restored, but we must be willing to take the steps necessary for things to be resolved and made right. Zacchaeus did this, too. He declared that anything he had taken deceitfully or under false pretenses from anyone would be restored four times over. Zacchaeus had some ground to reclaim, given his prior reputation. The Holy Spirit working in Zacchaeus's heart communicated to him that to live with integrity and wholeness, he needed to repair any pain his broken life had caused.

Restoration can be a hard thing to understand, but it is something that new and old generations alike must learn. We must recognize that, yes, when we repent of our sins, our record is cleansed in heaven. The righteousness of Christ is imputed to us. Our sins are cast away from God as far as the east is from the west, and we bear them no longer. We are forgiven, and it is just as if we had never sinned. Our relationship with our heavenly Father is restored; however, our earthly relationships may still be tainted by our previous failures and sins. In fact, many times, the horizontal damage our sins cause remains until we take the action necessary to heal and be restored.

Asking for forgiveness, returning stolen property, paying bad debts, repairing damaged relationships, going back to a spouse, or taking other steps may be needed to restore relationships and reclaim integrity. When we seek forgiveness and attempt to make amends, we are owning our sins. We are saying, "Yes, I was the one who did that wrong. And yes, this is me asking for forgiveness and wanting restoration." This bringing together the two halves of our divided lives by submitting our past and present to Christ establishes the moral ground for integrity that will allow us to influence others in our generation.

Gen Zers who live lives of integrity will be victorious over the enemy and will bring healing to our fractured world.

Without question, Generation Z will need great integrity for the days ahead as the leadership pressure on them increases exponentially. If their hearts are divided or if they are doing one thing while saying another, the pressures of the twenty-first century will crush them, and their houses will fall like the one built on the sand. However, if new generations learn the power of telling the truth, the freedom of true repentance, and the authority a life of purity commands, they can bring wholeness to our fractured world.

Gen Z was born *for* integrity *into* a world that needs it desperately. Gen Zers who live lives of integrity will be victorious over the enemy and will bring healing to our fractured world. They will join with vertically challenged Zacchaeus in welcoming Jesus into their homes and with David the psalmist in saying, "I know that you are pleased with me, for my enemy does not triumph over me. Because of my integrity you uphold me and set me in your presence forever."[189]

CHAPTER SEVEN
A GENERATION BORN FOR COMMITMENT: ZIPPORAH

One of the largest cast-bronze sculptures in America stands at the entrance to Oral Roberts University. This sixty-foot-tall, thirty-ton bronze work of art that looks similar to Albrecht Durer's famous praying hands is iconic. The hands were crafted in Mexico, shipped to the US, and originally installed in front of the City of Faith, a three-tower complex that stands directly across the street from the campus. Several decades ago, the hands were moved to the main entrance of the campus. Initially, the hands were known as the Healing Hands and represented the merging of prayer and medicine for the healing of man. For several years, this sculpture was the most visited tourist attraction in Tulsa, Oklahoma. On any given day, you will still find people from around the world stopping to get their picture taken in front of this spiritual symbol.

A few years ago, on the campus side of the sculpture, ORU created the "Wall of Sacrifice" to recognize alumni of the university who had given their lives in service for Christ. The names of several outstanding alumni grace the wall, including people like Dr. Myles Munroe, who died in a tragic plane crash while traveling to speak at a ministry conference. In the spring of 2019, ORU also commemorated the sacrifice of one of its most famous alumni by placing his name, John Allen Chau, on the wall. His sacrificial death well represents Generation Z's call and commitment to sharing Jesus with the world no matter the cost.

While John was attempting to reach the Sentinelese people with the gospel of Jesus Christ, some members of this indige-nous tribe killed him. The Sentinelese, whom many consider to be the most unreached group on earth, live on North Sentinel

Island, which is a small, isolated island in the Bay of Bengal that is governed by India. According to the Indian government, this tribe insists on living in complete isolation—no contact with the outside world. In fact, it is illegal in India to visit the Sentinelese people. They live without modern conveniences, healthcare, and any help or trade from other people groups. The Sentinelese have "no Bible in their language because no one else speaks their language, and no one has been able to get close enough to them to learn it... In many ways, North Sentinel Island is a human Jurassic Park, created and protected by the Indian government."[190]

It was in the fall of 2018 that John Chau embarked on a mission to share the message of Jesus' love with this isolated tribe, and he recorded his entire trip in his journal. An extensive article in *GQ* magazine reports that the morning before John set out for his final foray to the island, he wrote a letter to a close friend, saying, "'I think I might die... I'll see you again, bro—and remember, the first one to heaven wins.' The next day, the fishermen [who had dropped John off the day before] . . . motored along the coast, searching for signs of Chau. Eventually they spotted something on the beach. . . a body. . . being dragged by the Sentinelese, with a rope tied around its neck."[191] John did indeed give his life in an attempt to bring the good news of Jesus to unreached people. John's unique death brought a worldwide explosion of media engagement and, sad to say, criticism from some Christians. Once the initial barrage of negative media had circled the globe, a clearer story of John's commitment began to surface.

The story that emerged traced John's commitment to missions to his teenage years when he grew confident God was calling him to reach unreached peoples and, specifically, to reach the most unreached people on earth. As time passed, John discerned that this meant the North Sentinelese. During his life journey toward making the ultimate sacrifice for Christ, John attended ORU and graduated cum laude with a BS in Exercise Science. He was a wonderful, dedicated young man. He read mission-oriented books regularly and engaged in every training opportunity possible, including training his body for the rigors ahead.[192]

Following his death, as we closely reviewed John's journey to the mission field, "we realized that he may have been one of the most prepared missionaries ever [documented] as he engaged [in] an impossible task. He was also one of the most courageous. He understood that trying to reach the Sentinelese was dangerous and could mean his death. Yet, he went anyway."[193] A letter from John to his family highlighted the risks before him and the knowledge he had of those risks. He wrote this to his brother, sister, mom, and dad just before his last journey to North Sentinel Island.

Family,

You guys might think I'm crazy in all this, but I think it's worth it to declare Jesus to these people.

Please do not be angry at them or at God if I get killed. Rather please live your lives in obedience to whatever he has called you to and I'll see you again when you pass through the veil. "Don't retrieve my body."

This is not a pointless thing—the eternal lives of this tribe is at hand and I can't wait to see them around the throne of God worshipping in their own language as Revelation 7:9–10 states. I love you all and I pray none of you love anything in this world more than Jesus Christ.

Soli Deo Gloria
John Chau[194]

His brother and sister attended the "Wall of Sacrifice" ceremony at ORU where we unveiled John's name and celebrated his amazing life commitment. In my personal opinion, John Chau represents Generation Z not only in their desire to change the world but also in their willingness to do whatever is necessary to reach their generation for Christ. They are devoted and ready to sacrifice — even when it's hard.

In my personal opinion, John Chau represents Generation Z not only in their desire to change the world but also in their willingness to do whatever is necessary to reach their generation for Christ. They are devoted and ready to sacrifice— even when it's hard.

WHERE WILL THEY BURY YOUR HEART?

We know the name of David Livingstone as a famous missionary in Africa, but first, he sought confirmation of his call to the mission field. "By and by he asked whether I thought he would do for Africa. I said I believed he would, if he would not go to an old station but would advance to unoccupied ground, specifying the vast plain to the north where I had sometimes seen, in the morning sun, the smoke of a thousand villages where no missionary had ever been."[195] These words by famous African missionary Robert Moffatt struck the heart of young David Livingstone from Blantyre, Scotland. Livingstone's desire to be a missionary was directed toward Africa by the passion and work of Moffatt, so much so that Livingstone married Moffatt's daughter. Livingstone committed his life to Africa and to bringing the gospel to those villages and people who had never heard of Christ. Livingstone's calling pushed him into the deepest parts of the African bush, where he might go months or even years without being heard from by the outside world. When calling others to join him on the mission field, he would say, "If you have men who will only come if they know there is a good road, I don't want them. I want men who will come if there is no road at all."[196]

Livingstone traveled during very difficult and dangerous times. He walked more than twenty-nine-thousand miles, was mauled by a lion, contracted malaria on multiple occasions, was plagued by significant physical ailments, and was in constant danger from the Boers and tribes of the continent. He ultimately lost a child and a wife because of his mission work.[197] Yet Livingstone did not believe that his work was a sacrifice at all. He said, "People talk of the sacrifice I have made in spending so much of my life in Africa ... It is emphatically no sacrifice. Say rather it is a privilege."[198]

At one point, Livingstone was not heard from by the outside world for six years. The *New York Herald* newspaper sent Henry Stanley to find Livingstone, which he did, greeting him with these famous words: "Dr. Livingstone, I presume?" Stanley attempted to convince Livingstone, whose health was failing, to return to England, but Livingstone refused and continued to commit his life to African exploration and ministry. Shortly after telling Henry Stanley goodbye and refusing to return to England, and about a year before he died in 1873,[199] he wrote in his journal on his fifty-ninth birthday, "My birthday! My Jesus, my King, my Life, my All. I again dedicate my whole self to Thee."[200]

In early May 1873, Livingstone died on his knees, praying for Africa. Two of his ministry team members cut Livingstone's heart out of his body and buried it in African soil before returning the rest of his corpse to England.[201] Today, a monument stands near Chief Chitambo's Palace in Zambia, marking the spot where Livingstone's heart is buried. David Livingstone committed his life, emotions, and work to Africa, so it was fitting that his attendants buried his heart there. He is considered the greatest missionary in African history, and now, millions and millions of Christian believers live and thrive on this continent.

> **Generation Z is looking for and will find in Jesus a cause so compelling that it will require them to commit everything.**

Generation Z is looking for and will find in Jesus a cause so compelling that it will require them to commit everything. Every person in the world is looking for a cause, a reason, and a place where they can bury their heart and give all they possess for it. John Chau gave everything to reach the North Sentinelese, and David Livingstone committed his all to reach Africa. What about us? What about you? What is the cause or purpose God is calling *you* to? Are you willing to pay whatever price necessary to accomplish that mission and fulfill that cause?

Early church father Tertullian said, "The blood of the martyrs is the seed of the church."[202] From those first days following the resurrection of Jesus, His followers have suffered persecution and even death. He promised them that they would receive power, which would make them witnesses.[203] The word "witness" is translated from the Greek word *martus*, which is the same root word for "martyr."[204] In other words, the Holy Spirit would give them the power to become martyrs if necessary for the testimony of Jesus Christ. He will do the same for us today if we are willing to commit everything to the mission to which He is calling us.

ZIPPORAH

Our "Z" character for this chapter is Zipporah. Her story is one of a desert romance turned into a Lifetime drama. Zipporah must have wondered many times what she had gotten herself into by marrying Moses. Zipporah's first encounter with Moses was after he fled from the face of Pharaoh. Moses, though raised as an Egyptian, began to understand God's calling on his life and took things into his own hands, trying to deliver the people in his own strength. He murdered an Egyptian and then fled Egypt as a fugitive.

Moses' lonely journey northward out of Egypt led him into the land of the Midianites, who dwelt on the eastern side of the Jordan River on the Arabian Peninsula. The Midianites were descendants of Midian, who was the son of Abraham by his wife Keturah, so when Moses met the Midianites, he was meeting distant relatives through the family of Abraham. Moses rescued a group of young ladies who were being harassed by vagabonds at a watering hole and served them by ensuring their livestock were cared for. One of those young ladies was Zipporah, the seventh daughter of a Midianite named Jethro. Moses was invited into Jethro's home and ultimately given Zipporah to be his Midianite wife. Moses' romance with Zipporah began by rescuing a damsel in distress. For almost forty years, Moses and Zipporah lived in the desert of Midian with their two children, Gershom and Eliezer, while Moses shepherded the flocks of Jethro. Gershom might have been quite a bit older than his little brother Eliezer since their names are revealed many chapters apart in the book of Exodus.

When Moses encountered God at the burning bush and heard His call to return to Egypt, everything changed— including Zipporah's life. The life of a shepherd's wife is a long way from being the wife of a prophet, deliverer, and ruler of several million people. Moses' return to Egypt would move Zipporah from their calm, peaceful existence to the high drama of spiritual conflict. This must have been difficult for Zipporah. She had not personally seen the fire at the burning bush nor heard the voice of God. She had to trust her husband and his ability to hear God's voice clearly. Zipporah had never been to Egypt, and now she was being asked to participate in one of the greatest spiritual and physical confrontations in human history. Yet Zipporah must have also sensed that God's hand on Moses' life meant she was being called to play her part. She would commit to God's mission as much as Moses and become part of making history. But it would not be easy. True commitment never is.

In one of the more unusual passages in Scripture, we read about the commitment necessary to fulfill God's call in Egypt. Literally, on the way to Egypt with their two sons, Zipporah and Moses stopped at an inn to spend the night. On the road to fulfilling their calling, they encountered God at that inn in a most unusual way.

"At a lodging place on the way, the LORD met Moses and was about to kill him.

But Zipporah took a flint knife, cut off her son's foreskin and touched Moses' feet with it. 'Surely you are a bridegroom of blood to me,'[205] she said. So the LORD let him alone."[206]

When I first read this unusual passage years ago, I was stunned by those words—the "Lord was about to kill" Moses. Moses was called to return to Egypt, he was on a mission for God, and now the Lord was seeking to kill him. Why? This mysterious passage is not easy to understand. I believe that this was one of the tests that Moses and Zipporah were required to pass if they were to go to the next level of leadership. God would request a new level of self-crucifixion by Moses if he was going to lead God's people, and God would also require a new level of sacrifice by his family before allowing Moses to enter Egypt.

We are not sure how Zipporah discovered the Lord was trying to kill Moses or how she knew what needed to be done, but she discerned His will and responded accurately. In that moment of decision, Zipporah committed her family to the cause by transitioning her son from his Midianite heritage to a commitment as an Israelite. Zipporah took Gershom, and perhaps Eliezer as well, and circumcised him, throwing his foreskin at Moses' feet and calling Moses a bloody husband, which was not a compliment.

Commitments are not always a delight, but they are always necessary if we are going to fulfill our destiny and move forward in God's work. Moses would need to have his Gentile family fully committed as Israelites before going to announce that God had appointed him to bring deliverance to the Israelites. Moses was raised as a Gentile, but in this moment, his son would be initiated as a Hebrew. Zipporah saved Moses' life and made her commitment to being a fully Hebrew family with the children of Israel.

> **Commitments are not always a delight, but they are always necessary if we are going to fulfill our destiny and move forward in God's work.**

My wife, Lisa, has made numerous commitments during the years of our marriage. God's calling on my life has also meant God's calling on her life. She left her family behind and has gone with me across the nation and around the world. It has not always been easy. Many times, the spouse's commitment to ministry is more difficult and demanding than the minister's, but Lisa has made the necessary commitments. She has not only stood beside me but has also stood in her own right as a minister to thousands, serving as a spiritual mother and an example of godly commitment to the cause of Christ. Without Lisa's commitment to God's way, I could not have done what God has called me to do with my life. We have learned together that each successive leadership challenge has required increased commitment and sacrifice.

Generation Z will be called to make enormous commitments to the cause of Christ, some of which will be personally painful. Young Timothy was also required to make a painful commitment in order to join the apostle Paul's mission expedition.

Do What?

If an ad went out to college-aged students, or Generation Z young men in general, that they were being invited on the journey of a lifetime that would position them to change the world and make history, it would be received with significant excitement. However, if that same ad said in the fine print something like, "To join this effort, you will be required to have surgery on your sex organs, which may prove quite painful," then the number of respondents would be immediately reduced! For a young man, I cannot think of anything that would be a greater deterrent than to invite him into this kind of personal, intimate pain.

When Paul shared with Timothy what would be required to join his team, young Timothy must have thought to himself, "Do what?" Timothy loved the idea of ministering with Paul and traveling the world to preach Jesus. His heart leaped at this once-in-a-lifetime opportunity, but then the hammer (or should I say, "the knife") fell. To be part of Paul's team, he would need to allow Paul to perform an adult circumcision on him.[207] This meant that his most private part would suffer intense pain so that he could fulfill God's calling. Now, this was commitment!

Even more confusing was the fact that Paul was traveling from city to city, telling Gentile converts that they did not need to be circumcised to be Christians.[208] Even though Timothy's mother was Jewish, his father was Greek, so Timothy was not circumcised as a child.[209] Common logic would have said that because Timothy's father was a Gentile, Timothy would not need to be circumcised, according to the Jerusalem Council. However, God's requirements are not always logical, and it is always wise to obey them. Paul was requiring Timothy to be circumcised as a personal statement of his commitment to the cause. By being circumcised, Timothy would be received into the Hebrew community and have greater authority to tell the Hebrew Christians that the Gentiles did not need to be circumcised. So, Timothy made the deep, intimate commitment necessary to become a missionary on Paul's team and would, of course, become a great minister himself. [210]

> **Generation Z will be called to make commitments beyond other generations in order to do what they have not done.**

Generation Z will be called to make commitments beyond other generations in order to do what they have not done. For this to happen, they will need to remove all limits to their commitment level. They will need to remove the geographical boundaries. I have good friends whose impact on the world has been reduced because they told God they were not moving from their home, no matter what the opportunity. God still loves and blesses these geographically bound friends to some extent, but their life impact has been dwarfed by this artificial restriction.

Gen Zers will also need to remove the financial boundaries. Many times, young people want to start at the top of the pay scale and expect to be treated like they have years of experience and expertise when they are just beginning. My advice to them and you would be never to restrict your response to God's call due to financial considerations. I have watched over and over as people said "no" to doors God was opening for them because they were making more money in the current job—only to see that job disappear after a few years—or even a few days. Then, there they were without the money, but most importantly, without the satisfaction, joy, and eternal reward of doing God's will. No place should be too low or too high for us concerning following our Master. Take the limits off!

Generation Z, like Zipporah, her son, and young Timothy, is being asked to make personal and intimate commitments to God's call at the deepest levels. These painful declarations of allegiance will be rewarded with amazing victories and the opportunity to be part of the greatest spiritual drama in human history that will take place as we progress through the twenty-first century. Circumcision of the flesh can represent a circumcision of the heart, a spiritual death that allows us to fully live for Christ.

Paul informed the Roman believers that "A person is not a Jew who is one only outwardly, nor is circumcision merely outward and physical. No, a person is a Jew who is one inwardly; and circumcision is circumcision of the heart, by the Spirit, not by the written code. Such a person's praise is not from other people, but from God."[211] Later, possibly writing from a Roman prison, Paul reminded the Colossians of this: "In him you were also circumcised with a circumcision not performed by human hands. Your whole self ruled by the flesh was put off when you were circumcised by Christ."[212]

Commitment to God's cause may be uncomfortable and might seem unfair. In fact, I can promise that it will be at times. What God requires may even cause us deep, personal, and intimate pain, but the work of God is worth all pain or sacrifice required. The pain we experience now positions us for the progress we will experience tomorrow. The pain is all about our progress.

> **What God requires may even cause us deep, personal, and intimate pain, but the work of God is worth all pain or sacrifice required.**
> **—Livingstone**

In his book titled *Spiritual Leadership*, J. Oswald Sanders shared a poem by an unknown author that helps us to understand this:

> *When God wants to drill a man*
> *and thrill a man*
> *and skill a man*
> *When God wants to mold a man*
> *To play the noblest part;*
> *When he yearns with all his heart*
> *To create so great and bold a man*
> *That all the world shall be amazed,*
> *Watch his methods, watch his ways!*

How he ruthlessly perfects
Whom he royally elects!
How he hammers him and hurts him,
And with mighty blows converts him
Into trial shapes of clay which
Only God understands;
While his tortured heart is crying
And he lifts beseeching hands!
How he bends but never breaks
When his good he undertakes;
How he uses whom he chooses
And with every purpose fuses him;
By every act induces him
To try his splendor out —
God knows what he is about.[213]

God does know what He is about. The commitment of John Chau, David Livingstone, Timothy, and Zipporah teaches us that God's will is worth the sacrifice. Livingstone would say this:

There is one safe and happy place, and that is in the will of God.. . . If a commission by an earthly king is considered an honor, how can a commission by a Heavenly King be considered a sacrifice?. . . Away with the word sacrifice. Say rather it is a privilege. Anxiety, sickness, suffering, or danger, now and then, with a foregoing of the common conveniences and charities of this life, may make us pause, and cause the spirit to waver, and the soul to sink; but let this only be for a moment. All these are nothing when compared with the glory which shall be revealed in and for us. I never made a sacrifice.[214]

Generation Z is following the millennial generation, also known as Generation Y, whose struggle to make commitments has been epic. Employers of millennials have learned that loyalty and commitment regarding the workplace have been a huge issue. Gallup recently called millennials the "job-hopping generation," noting that 21 percent of millennials say they have changed jobs in the last year, which is three times the number of non-millennials who responded the same.[215] On the other hand, Generation Z is looking for a place where they can make a longer-term commitment though they still have a huge desire to be their own boss. Yet, they are more settled and pragmatic than their predecessors. This desire to commit can and must be translated into committing to God's work and making the needed sacrifices to fulfill God's plan for their lives. May all of us reading this chapter ensure that the knife of God's Word is applied to our fleshly hearts once again as we enter the next exciting phase of God's work in our lives. And, years from now, may Generation Z be known as a generation of commitment!

CHAPTER EIGHT
A GENERATION BORN FOR INFLUENCE: ZERUIAH

"Leadership is influence, nothing more, nothing less."[216] If this statement by *The New York Time*s best-selling author and speaker John Maxwell is close to being true, then the leadership potential of Generation Z is huge because they are influencing the world. Generation Z is now the largest generation on the planet, as 2.47 billion of the 7.8 billion people on earth are part of it. Larger than both the millennial and baby boomer generations, Generation Z's number alone positions them to make a significant impact. [217]

Gen Z is currently influencing consumer and financial decisions in a substantial way. *Forbes* magazine recently noted that Gen Z represents \$29–143 billion in buying power in the United States, along with exhibiting a considerable influence on how monies are spent by other generations. "Ninety-three percent of parents today say their children influence family and household purchases, according to a report by CASSANDRA, meaning a major portion of overall market spend is because of these youths."[218] Marketers and businesses are acutely aware of Gen Z's buying and decision-making power and are attempting to identify what works with them. The traits that characterize Generation Z can be surprising, combining a desire for security, authenticity, and social value with an expectation of speed, convenience, and seamless service.[219]

A recent McKinsey report says Gen Zers are undefined, communaholics, prologuers, and realistic. They are also a

> Generation Z is now the largest generation on the planet, as 2.47 billion of the 7.8 billion people on earth are part of it.

consumer force to be reckoned with, according to McKinsey, who states, "Young people have always embodied the zeitgeist of their societies, profoundly influencing trends and behavior alike. The influence of Gen Z—the first generation of true digital natives—is now radiating outward, with the search for truth at the center of its characteristic behavior and consumption patterns. Technology has given young people an unprecedented degree of connectivity among themselves and with the rest of the population. That makes generational shifts more important and speeds up technological trends as well."[220]

Generation Z is also more financially conservative than other generations. Michael Pankowski, who leads the Crimson Connection on the Harvard campus and is a Gen Zer himself, said, "35% of us plan to start saving for retirement in our 20s, and another 10% are planning to save as teens."[221]

Over the next decade, their influence and leadership on social issues from climate change to abortion will be felt in the capitals of the world.

Generation Z is also influencing nations and politics. Roughly 24 million Gen Zers were eligible to vote in the 2020 election, which accounted for roughly 10 percent of the total number of eligible voters in the US.[222] Generation Z has been at the forefront of protests against racism around the world, and they are the most racially diverse generation ever. They will overthrow and reverse systemic racism patterns, opting for societies where every race and mixtures of races are treated equally. Over the next decade, their influence and leadership on social issues from climate change to abortion will be felt in the capitals of the world.

Generation Z will also lead and influence the world because of their educational prowess. They will be the most educated generation in history. A recent Pew Research Analysis noted that more Generation Zers are in college in the United States at the age of eighteen to twenty-one years than were in any previous generation at the same age.[223] These trends are also true globally as the emerging middle class accesses higher education, bringing an explosive need for advanced opportunities while giving rise to a host of new global institutions to meet the need. This ascendant knowledge base in Gen Z will serve them well in the marketplace and push them toward leadership quickly.

Generation Z's technology capacity and savvy will serve to escalate and expedite their influence. They are the first digital natives with many of them learning to operate a smartphone before they learned to walk. According to a 2018 Pew Research Center survey, 95 percent of thirteen- to seventeen-year-olds have access to a smartphone, and a similar share (97 percent) use at least one of seven major online platforms. YouTube, Instagram, and Snapchat are among teens' favorite online destinations. Some 85 percent say they use YouTube, 72 percent use Instagram, and 69 percent use Snapchat. Some 45 percent of teens say they are online "almost constantly," and an additional 44 percent say they are online several times a day.[224] Gen Z will continue to find ways to turn their online presence into progress. For instance, the highest-paid YouTuber in the world is eight-year-old toy reviewer Ryan Kaji, who makes $26 million a year from his channel Ryan ToysReview, now known as Ryan's World.[225]

Gen Z will influence the world. This is indisputable. However, the question before us and them is *how* will they influence it? This collective generation has the greatest opportunity in the history of humankind to make a positive impact and an exponentially expanded opportunity to grow the influence of God's kingdom on the earth. I believe that they are the new leadership generation, and everyone will see their impact for good in the days ahead.

Young Leaders

Jesus chose young people as leaders. Some scholars believe that most of the apostles were anywhere from their early twenties to early thirties when Jesus chose and commissioned them to do His work.[226] Throughout Christian history, great movements of God have consistently been led by young men and women.

For instance, the great Welsh revival of 1904 was led by Evan Roberts. During this revival, more than 100,000 people were converted to Christ in just over one year, with the entire country of Wales being transformed by the power of God.[227] Jails were emptied, court dockets lay dormant, bars were closed for lack of clientele, and divorces were negligible.[228] Even the donkeys that were used to work in the mines were confused by the revival. They were so accustomed to hearing the miners curse them during their work that when the miners ceased cursing because their

> **Gen Z will influence the world. This is indisputable. However, the question before us and them is *how* will they influence it?**

lives were changed by Christ, the donkeys did not know what commands to obey![229]

The revival that swept across Wales in waves of power and conversion had its epicenter in young people and youth gatherings. Most people trace the initial spark of the revival to a youth meeting held in New Quay where one young lady, Florrie Evans, stood to testify and proclaimed from her pure spirit, "I love the Lord Jesus with all my heart." Conviction fell and young people began confessing their sins, forming the groundswell of what was to come. During this time, Evan Roberts, a young evangelist in his twenties, spoke at a youth gathering in Lougher, Wales. It was a small crowd, but God's presence was strong. Within days, the crowds grew and gathered to seek God fervently.[230] Roberts outlined four points in his early messages that would form the basis for the revival:

1. Confess all known sin, receiving forgiveness through Jesus Christ.
2. Remove anything in your life that you are in doubt or feel unsure about.
3. Be ready to obey the Holy Spirit instantly.
4. Publicly confess the Lord Jesus Christ.

These themes continued throughout the revival and became foundational to what God did in Wales. Roberts quickly became the leader of the revival and noted that God had touched him dramatically before the revival began. During the prayer movement leading up to the revival, Roberts was touched by the Holy Spirit and cried out, "Lord, bend me!"[231] Roberts was offering his life to God to be shaped and influenced by the divine, to be bent in the direction of heaven. Roberts and all of Wales discovered that when God shapes your life, He can use you to shape the world around you.

Roberts had a vision of 100,000 people being converted to Christ in Wales before the revival ever began. During 1904–5, Roberts became a national and global influencer. His leadership was unsurpassed in the nation. God entrusted him in his early twenties to lead this dramatic outpouring that would become the precursor to the Azusa Street revival in Los Angeles and the Spirit-empowered movement around the world. When Roberts died in 1951, his obituary summarized his life well by saying, "He was a man who had experienced strange things. In his youth, he had seemed to hold the nation in the palms of his hands."[232]

Generation Z has the potential to hold nations in the palms of their hands as they allow God to bend and shape them for His glory

Like young Evan Roberts, Generation Z has the potential to hold nations in the palms of their hands as they allow God to bend and shape them for His glory. The private visions the Holy Spirit is birthing in young hearts will become visible in our day. During the twenty-first century, we will witness young leaders rising to lead great moves of the Holy Spirit in the world. Churches, cities, regions, nations, and entire continents will be impacted as they make spiritual history. We will also see young men and women impact the systems of the world in new ways.

A Stand for Justice

Born Michael King Jr., one man in his youth became the most notable leader in the American civil rights movement. He was born into a preacher's home. His dad, Michael King Sr., became the pastor of Ebenezer Baptist Church in Atlanta, Georgia, in 1931, when his son was just two years old. Michael's name was later changed to Martin Luther King Jr. In the years ahead, this young leader's influence would be felt around the world in his generation as it is still being felt to this day.[233]

Martin studied in Atlanta, Pennsylvania, and Boston, ultimately obtaining his doctorate in 1955.[234] In this same year, he was called to pastor the Dexter Avenue Baptist Church in Montgomery, Alabama.[235] It was there that the twenty-six-year-old King began to emerge as the face of civil rights protests in America—leading the Montgomery Bus Boycotts and becoming president of the Southern Christian Leadership Conference.[236][237] King's leadership in nonviolent protests and civil disobedience gave voice and direction to the energies of Black Americans yearning for equal rights and the overthrow of segregation, enshrined in the separate-but-equal laws across the nation. The Christian values undergirding King's leadership and his adoption of Mahatma Gandhi's nonviolent methods for initiating change became the earmarks of his leadership.

King helped organize the 1963 March on Washington, where he delivered his famous "I Have a Dream" speech on the steps of the Lincoln Memorial.[238] Perhaps no single speech by any leader of his generation had a greater or more long-lasting effect than this visionary declaration of the dream residing in the hearts of millions of Americans: that we could

all live free and equal. It is one of the great oratory master-
pieces of all time. Amazingly, King was only thirty-four years
of age when he gave this speech. On October 14, 1964, he won
the Nobel Peace Prize for combating racial inequality through
nonviolent resistance and became the youngest Nobel winner
up to that time. [239] [240]

The Civil Rights Act of 1964 outlawed discrimination based
on race, color, religion, sex, or national origin and prohibited
unequal application of voter registration requirements and
racial segregation in schools, employment, and public accom-
modations.[241] The Voting Rights Act of 1965 prohibited racial
discrimination in voting.[242] Both of these landmark rulings in
America can be attributed to King's leadership.

In April 1968, Martin Luther King, Jr., was assassinated
at a Memphis hotel the day after delivering his prophetic "I've
Been to the Mountaintop" speech at Mason Temple, the head-
quarters church of the Church of God in Christ denomination.
[243] His death set off a firestorm of protests and grief across the
nation and around the world. Shortly after his death, the Civil
Rights Act of 1968, commonly known as the Fair Housing Act,
was signed into law—another tribute to King's tireless efforts
for racial equality.

In 1983, President Ronald Reagan signed a law creating
Martin Luther King Jr., Day as a national holiday in the US.[244]
This holiday is celebrated each year on the third Monday of
January. King died before his fortieth birthday, having influenced an entire nation for generations to come. The battle
for equality continues in America, but the strides made in
the 1950s and 1960s continue to serve as a source of hope
for oppressed people around the world. This young leader's

influential words continue to inspire. Here are a few of my favorite quotes from Dr. King.

- "A genuine leader is not a searcher for consensus but a molder of consensus."
- "Not everybody can be famous, but everybody can be great because greatness is determined by service ... You only need a heart full of grace and a soul generated by love."
- "We may have all come on different ships, but we're in the same boat now."
- "I have decided to stick with love. Hate is too great a burden to bear."
- "If you can't fly then run, if you can't run then walk, if you can't walk then crawl, but whatever you do you have to keep moving forward."
- "A man who won't die for something is not fit to live."
- "I have a dream that my four little children will one day live in a nation where they will not be judged by the color of their skin, but by the content of their character."
- "I refuse to accept the view that mankind is so tragically bound to the starless midnight of racism and war that the bright daybreak of peace and brotherhood can never become a reality. . . I believe that unarmed truth and unconditional love will have the final word."[245]

Generation Z also carries a passion for social justice and equality around the globe. They are the most diverse generation in history and simply do not look at the issues of equality the way other generations have. To them, racial equality should be a given, and when it is not, they seek ways to make a difference. During the 2020 coronavirus pandemic, racial riots exploded across America and around the world in protest of police brutality and senseless killings with racial overtones. Once again, the pressure against systemic, racial prejudice surfaced, calling for further and deeper action.

> I have decided to stick with love. Hate is too great a burden to bear.
> —*Martin Luther King Jr.*

Yubo polled 38,919 US-based Gen Zers (those ages thirteen to twenty-five) in early June 2020 and found that 88 percent of respondents believe Black Americans are treated differently than others. Seventy-seven percent of respondents had already attended a protest to support equality for Black Americans, and 62 percent said they were willing to get arrested during a peaceful protest to support this equality. Furthermore, 86 percent felt that peaceful protests and political demonstrations are necessary to create a significant change.[246]

> They are the most diverse generation in history and simply do not look at the issues of equality the way other generations have.

Generation Z is not afraid or hesitant to make their voices heard or influence known, whether on campus or in the public square. They are passionate about justice and want substantial authentic change. When this influence is applied around the world, it will bring significant upheaval to the current order of things. As it was said of Evan Roberts, they will hold the nations in the palms of their hands. Generation Z will be influential. Yet, much of this influence will be a nameless, faceless influence by masses more than by one individual or leader. The flatness of our world and access to media by the Gen Z billions will allow them to lead change and influence the world, albeit somewhat anonymously. Spiritually, they will join the hundreds of people in biblical history who made a big difference in shaping the world, but whose names we never knew, or at least never heard much about.

ZERUIAH

Our "Z" influencer for this chapter is a lady named Zeruiah, who was a sister to King David. Zeruiah was an observer as God raised her brother to prominence in Israel. She saw the initial oil of anointing run down from his head. She cheered as Goliath fell. She sang with other Israelite maidens as Philistines were defeated, and she prayed as the threats of Saul were overcome. What a proud day it was for his sister when David was finally anointed and accepted as king of Judah and later as king of united Israel! This was her *brother*, God's chosen king. The transition from the sister of a shepherd boy to the sister of a king was exciting. What a journey, what an honor, and what an opportunity to make an impact. Zeruiah found herself in a place of influence because of the timing of her birth and family connection, and she used this influence for good.

Members of Generation Z, like Zeruiah, are being given an opportunity for influence and leadership because of the timing of their birth. They are alive during these exciting days at the end of an age. They were not aborted, have not committed suicide, and are not overwhelmed by the darkness surrounding them. They are here and ready to bring their voices and influence for and to the King. Zeruiah had King David's ear, and this generation has the ear of our heavenly King Jesus. Christ's heart is toward them, and He is prepared to listen to their pleas.

In Zeruiah's case, her influence came mostly through her sons, Abishai, Joab, and Asahel. All three of these young men found a place in David's army, with all of them named among David's mighty men. They were warriors for the king. Scripture teaches that children are like arrows in the hands of a warrior.[247] Zeruiah pointed these arrows—her greatest resource, her sons—at both the physical and spiritual enemies of the king.

Zeruiah's oldest son, Abishai, was a stellar member of the king's team. He was close to David and served with him during the wilderness days of fleeing from Saul. He became a commander of one of the three divisions of David's army and personally killed three hundred of the enemy in one battle and saved David's life when the giant Ishbi-benob attempted to kill him. He also helped kill David's rebellious son, Absalom. Zeruiah's middle son, Joab, was one of the more famous military leaders in the Bible, ultimately becoming the general of David's army. He led the charge to take Jerusalem as David's capital and was the king's closest confidant over the years. Joab's influence in military conquests during the days of David's reign was inestimable. The expansion of David's kingdom was led by Joab; he was a fierce and, at times, brutal warrior during the golden years of kingdom expansion. Joab did not finish well, as he did not transfer his loyalty to David's successor, Solomon. However, Zeruiah's middle son was among the mightiest of the mighty men.

The youngest son, Asahel, was the least prominent of the three in David's army, but he was still named among his thirty mighty men. Asahel was swift afoot—a fast runner. He was killed by Abner in a battle with the sons of Saul.[248]

Scripture is filled with people who had great influence but were not popular or well-known. In many instances, their names are not even recorded in Scripture even though they did amazing things or saw significant miracles.

I have never heard a message or teaching on this influential "Z" woman. Zeruiah is there in Scripture, but she remains relatively anonymous. Her name is not proclaimed or lauded by anyone, yet her influence was mighty. Through her children, Zeruiah may have done as much or more than any other person in the Bible to extend the kingdom of God's anointed. Zeruiah used the timing of her birth, her access to the king, and the arrows (children) God put in her hand, to influence God's work and His Kingdom. Zeruiah did this from a place of relative obscurity but a place of great influence nonetheless. Generation Z can do the same.

Scripture is filled with people who had great influence but were not popular or well-known. In many instances, their names are not even recorded in Scripture even though they did amazing things or saw significant miracles. People like the woman at the well, the Shunamite woman, the woman who poured oil on Jesus' head, and the servant lady who pointed Naaman toward the prophet Elisha, who could heal his leprosy. These were mighty women whose names we will never know.

Others in this "famous unknown" category might include the man healed by Peter and John at the temple, the little boy who loaned Jesus his lunch so the Master could feed five thousand, or the four men who carried a paralytic onto a rooftop and lowered him down in front of Jesus so he could be healed. Over and over again, people who performed great exploits and were used dramatically by God in the scriptural narratives are not called by name. In my personal opinion, this pattern will be seen more and more in these tumultuous days. In a world where Gen Zers are their own publishers, and the media platforms of the world are flooded with information, we will see millions of young people be used to make a significant and eternal impact without the masses ever knowing their names. Like Zeruiah, they will use their places of influence with the King to change the world and expand His kingdom.

Generation Influence

The more I study Generation Z, the more I am convinced that their leadership positions in the world will be great. And if leadership is influence (I personally believe leadership is more than just influence, but it does *include* influence), then the impact of their leadership will be amazing. One name for them could be *Generation Influence* because the persuasiveness they will exert on the world in the days ahead will be astronomical.

Denominations and church networks are giving more and more attention to Generation Z because they understand the influence they will have. One teenager excited about Jesus can awaken an entire church and spark renewal and revival as seen in the Welsh revival. Generation Z will change and influence the church dramatically. As they lead, we should expect high-tech with simplicity, biblical truth with great storytelling, global connectivity with local mentoring, supernatural experience with natural expressions, lifestyle evangelism with bold and prophetic proclamations, deep questioning with courageous faith, and new levels of acceptance for everyone, along with a willingness to sacrifice whatever it takes for the cause of Christ. I am excited about the trends I see among today's generation, especially concerning the influence they will have on the church. Old systems will be transformed by the impact of this leadership generation, and the greatest harvest in the history of the world will be the result. Generation Influence is here, and their leadership will be felt and seen mightily within the church.

Tomorrow's presidents, prime ministers, educators, business leaders, scientists, medical leaders, artists, inventors, researchers, conveners, and cultural missionaries are currently in classrooms around the world (or maybe somewhere in a corner playing video games).

Gen Z will also influence and lead the world. Tomorrow's presidents, prime ministers, educators, business leaders, scientists, medical leaders, artists, inventors, researchers, conveners, and cultural missionaries are currently in classrooms around the world (or maybe somewhere in a corner playing video games). They will emerge better equipped and more capable than most any generation of leaders ever. Gen Z will quickly overtake others as they exert their influence on the world. If this new generation allows God to bend them and shape them, our world will be better because of their leadership. If they resist or turn away from Him, their leadership will push the world toward destruction.

The stakes have never been higher. May God help all of us as we encourage, minister to, and love Gen Z: Generation of Influence.

CONCLUSION

The sawdust crunched beneath my knees as I knelt at the rough-hewn altar. The first night of youth camp ended with an invitation for prayer, and I was one of the first people to go forward. Just a few weeks earlier, I had surrendered to Jesus and committed to attend my first-ever Christian retreat. Now, as I knelt quietly, the presence of God surrounded me and flooded my being. My teenage encounter with God that night would mark my life forever. I would never be the same. Even now, as I reflect on the profound difference the work of the Holy Spirit has made in my journey for more than forty-five years, I am humbled, grateful, and amazed. The entire trajectory and direction of these years have been guided and informed by the Holy Spirit in profound ways. Thank God for that youth camp altar moment and for the thousands of moments I have had with the Holy Spirit since that summer night.

My own life is a testimony of what happens when a young person encounters God and is filled with the Holy Spirit. Destiny is formed and history is made. Since that "Spirit in the sawdust" meeting, much of my life has been given to reaching and touching young people. I guess this is natural since my life was so profoundly touched at a youth gathering. From local church youth work to statewide efforts, to global denominational ministry, to pastoring, to network-building, and finally, to a university president, I have always been drawn to investing in the next generation. I have started youth conferences and international camping efforts, led mission teams and youth evangelism outreaches, designed youth mentoring retreats and discipleship efforts, taped television shows and produced videos, hosted focus groups and launched systems, and attempted almost any other activity I could dream of that might touch new generations for God. Whether that new generation has been Generation X, millennials, or now Gen Z, each successive generation has brought new challenges and new potential.

From all my years of travel and engagement with young people, I have become convinced that Gen Z is special and unique. The unprecedented variables surrounding them have created an environment conducive to greatness. I believe they will rise to the occasion and that history will view them as one of the most important generations to ever live. In *Generation Z: Born for the Storm*, I have attempted to help all of us, including the Gen Zers who have made it this far in the book (or who are reading the conclusion first), to understand their immense potential. I do not claim to understand Gen Z completely, but I do proclaim that I love and believe in them completely.

The dark, foreboding clouds of difficulty continue to swirl even as I conclude this volume. The storms are going to be strong in the days ahead, and Jesus is going to be revealed in mighty ways. Above the wars, disasters, calamities, diseases, and difficulties, however, Christ will stand—calling our names and beckoning us to step onto the surface of the sea and walk with Him. I believe that many in Gen Z are standing on the edge of a boat right now with their faces turned into the wind or kneeling in the sawdust at a makeshift altar somewhere— giving Jesus everything. Fearless and faith-filled, they are about to make history. Their time of destiny has come, and the Holy Spirit has marked them for this moment. My heart sees them as they believe God's estimation of them and as they step onto the sea, witnessing the miraculous. The depth of the storm before us will only make the height of their victory appear even greater. When the dust of time has settled and tumult has turned into eternal peace, it will be forever known that Generation Z was *Born for the Storm.*

ABOUT THE AUTHOR

Dr. Billy Wilson is the president of Oral Roberts University in Tulsa, Oklahoma, and the global co-chair for Empowered21, a network helping to shape the future of the Spirit-empowered movement throughout the world. He is also chair for Pentecostal World Fellowship and a member of the board of the National Association of Evangelicals. Wilson served as the executive officer for the 2006 Azusa Street Centennial, which drew together over fifty thousand people from 112 nations to celebrate the hundredth anniversary of the Azusa Street Revival. A global influencer and dynamic speaker, Wilson is also the author of Father Cry and Fasting Forward, as well as the television host of World Impact with Billy Wilson. Billy and his wife Lisa reside in Tulsa, Oklahoma, where they enjoy spending time with their two children and six grandchildren.

ENDNOTES

INTRODUCTION A PERFECT STORM

1   Sebastian Junger, The Perfect Storm: A True Story of Men against the Sea (New York: W.W. Norton & Company, Inc., 1997).

2   Michael Dimock, "Defining Generations: Where Millennials End and Generation Z Begins," Pew Research Center, January 17, 2019, https://www.pewresearch.org/fact-tank/2019/01/17/where-millennials-end-and-generation-z-begins/.

CHAPTER ONE A GENERATION BORN TO LEAD: "ZEKE"

3   Jean Twenge, iGen: Why Today's Super-Connected Kids Are Growing Up Less Rebellious, More Tolerant, Less Happy—And Completely Unprepared for Adulthood—And What That Means for the Rest of Us (New York: Atria Books, 2017), 10.

4   History.com Editors, "This Day in History: November 22—President John F. Kennedy Is Assassinated," last updated November 19, 2019, https://www.history.com/this-day-in-history/john-f-kennedy-assassinated.

5   Hannah Ritchie et al., "Terrorism," Our World in Data, revised November 2019, https://ourworldindata.org/terrorism.

6   American Psychological Association, "Stress in America: Generation Z," Stress in America Survey (Washington DC: APA, 2018), 2, https://www.apa.org/news/press/releases/stress/2018/stress-gen-z.pdf.

7   Bonnie Berkowitz et al., "More and Deadlier: Mass Shooting Trends in America," The Washington Post, August 5, 2019, https://www.washingtonpost.com/nation/2019/08/05/more-deadlier-mass-shooting-trends-america/.

8   Philip Bump, "Eighteen Years of Gun Violence in U.S. Schools, Mapped," The Washington Post, February 14, 2018, https://www.washingtonpost.com/news/politics/wp/2018/02/14/eighteen-years-of-gun-violence-in-u-s-schools-mapped/.

9   Umair Irfan and Brian Resnick, "Megadisasters Devastated America in 2017. And They're Only Going to Get Worse," Vox, updated March 26, 2018, https://www.vox.com/energy-and-environment/2017/12/28/16795490/natural-disasters-2017-hurricanes-wildfires-heat-climate-change-cost-deaths.

10 "Deadly Diseases: Epidemics throughout History," CNN, October 2014, https://www.cnn.com/interactive/2014/10/health/epidemics-through-history/.

11 Information current as of May 25, 2021 from "Coronavirus Pandemic (COVID-19) – the data," Our World in Data, Statistics and Research, https://ourworldindata.org/coronavirus-data.

12 Lk 21:11

13 Lk 21:25–26

14 Mt 24:7–13

15 Mt 24:14

16 Is 40:30–31

17 Martin Gilbert, Churchill: The Power of Words (London, UK: Bantam Press, 2013), 312.

18 Derek Thomas, God Strengthens: Ezekiel Simply Explained (Darlington, UK: EP Books, 2014).

19 The Editors of Encyclopaedia Britannica, "Ezekiel," Encyclopaedia Britannica, November 16, 2009, https://www.britannica.com/biography/Ezekiel-Hebrew-prophet.

20 Ez 1:4

21 Ez 2:1–2

22 Original map. Information taken from map in Jefferson White, "Paul's Voyage to Rome and Shipwreck," in Evidence and Paul's Journeys: An Historical Investigation into the Travels of the Apostle Paul (self-published, 2019), available at https://jeffersonwhite.com/pauls-journeys/pauls-shipwreck-1/.

23 Acts 27:10

24 Michael Powell, "In 9/11 Chaos, Giuliani Forged a Lasting Image," New York Times, September 21, 2007, https://www.nytimes.com/2007/09/21/us/politics/21giuliani.html.

25 Acts 27:22–24

26 Acts 27:31

27 Alex Sanfilippo, "A Leader Is One Who Knows the Way, Goes the Way, and Shows the Way," DailyPS, May 23, 2019, https://dailyps.com/a-leader-is-one-who-knows-the-way-goes-the-way-and-shows-the-way/.

28 Acts 27:34

29 "Christian History: John Wesley," Christianity Today, accessed November 26, 2020, https://www.christianitytoday.com/history/people/denominationalfounders/john-wesley.html.

30 Joe Iovino, "Holy Spirit Moments: Learning from Wesley at Aldersgate," UMC, May 18, 2017, https://www.umc.org/en/content/holy-spirit-moments-learning-from-wesley-at-aldersgate.

31 Is 26:3–4

32 Acts 28:4–5

33 Acts 28:8–9

34 Mt 14:22–26

35 Mt 14:27–29

CHAPTER TWO A GENERATION BORN FOR A
PURPOSE: ZAPHENATH-PANEAH

36 Thomas M. Koulopoulos and Dan Keldsen, The Gen Z Effect: The 6 Forces
Shaping the Future of Business (Brookline, MA: Bibliomotion, 2014), 7.

37 Zach Mercurio, "Think Millennials Are Purpose-Driven? Meet Generation
Z," HuffPost, November 28, 2017, https://www.huffpost.com/entry/think-mil-
lennials-are-purpose-driven-meet generation_b_5a1da9f3e4b04f26e4ba9499.

38 Mercurio, "Think Millennials Are Purpose-Driven?"

39 Sparks and Honey, "Meet Generation Z: Forget Everything You Learned
about Millennials," slide presentation, posted on June 17, 2014, SlideShare,
https://www.slideshare.net/sparksandhoney/generation-z-final-june-17.

40 The Change Generation Report: How Millennials and Gen Z Are Redefining
Work (Ontario, Canada: Lovell Corporation, 2017), 9, available to download
at BridgingTheGap, https://bridgingthegapventures.com/the-change-genera-
tion-report/.

41 "Getting to Know Generation Z: The Desire for Purpose and Fulfillment,"
Competitive Solutions, Inc., accessed February 18, 2020, http://csipbl.com/
getting-know-generation-z-desire-purpose-fulfillment/.

42 Shane Pruitt, "10 Characteristics of Generation Z," ChurchLeaders, September 21, 2017, https://churchleaders.com/outreach-missions/outreach-mis-
sions-articles/310160-10-characteristics-generation-z-shane-pruitt.html.

43 Acts 13:36

44 Gn 41:45–46

45 International Standard Bible Encyclopedia, s.v. "Zaphnath-Paaneah," Bible
Hub, accessed April 10, 2021, https://biblehub.com/topical/z/zaphnath-paa-
neah.htm.

46 Easton's Bible Dictionary, s.v. "Zaphnath-Paaneah," Bible Hub, accessed
April 23, 2020, https://biblehub.com/topical/z/zaphnath-paaneah.htm.

47 Mt 4:1–11

48 Dale Kuehne, "Q Moments: What Does It Mean to Be Made in the Image
of God?," video, 1:00, Qideas, accessed October 15, 2020, https://qideas.org/
qmoments/what-does-it-mean-to-be-made-in-the-image-of-god/.

49 Nancy R. Gibbs, et al., "Time Archive: Where Are All the Fathers?,"
Time, June 16, 2007, http://content.time.com/time/magazine/arti-
cle/0,9171,978762,00.html.

50 "Summary of Study Findings: Fathering in America," National Center for
Fathering, May 2009, https://fathers.com/wp39/wp-content/uploads/
2007/04/2009_Fathering_in_America_Summary.pdf.

51 Billy Wilson, Father Cry: Healing Your Heart and the Hearts of Those You
Love (Minneapolis: Chosen, 2012).

52 Gn 37:3

53 Is 61

54 Gal 3:27

55 Mi 6:8

56 Rom 8:28–29

57 Acts 9:17–18

58 1 Sm 16:13

59 Lk 4:17–21

60 "Road to First Flight," National Park Service, accessed February 18, 2020, https://www.nps.gov/articles/roadtofirstflight.htm.

61 "'We Choose to Go to the Moon': JFK's Moon Shot," Smithsonian National Air and Space Museum, December 12, 2017, https://airandspace.si.edu/stories/editorial/we-choose-go-moon-jfks-moon-shot.

62 Friedrich Nietzsche, quoted in Victor Frankl, Man's Search for Meaning (Boston: Beacon Press, 2006), 76.

63 Billy Nilles, "20 Fascinating Facts about Jim Carrey," E! News, February 9, 2020, https://www.eonline.com/news/1121005/20-fascinating-facts-about-jim-carrey#photo-283515.

64 Matt Crump, "Resilience and the Great Bounce Back," Matt Crump (website), June 21, 2018, https://mattcrump.tv/2018-6-21-resilience-and-the-great-bounce-back/.

65 Gal 6:9

66 1 Cor 6:18

67 2 Tm 2:22

68 M. G. Easton, Illustrated Bible Dictionary, 3rd ed (Nashville: Thomas Nelson, 1897), s.v. "Ephraim."

69 Easton, Illustrated Bible Dictionary, s.v. "Manasseh."

70 Gn 50:25

71 Heb 11:22

CHAPTER THREE A GENERATION BORN TO WORSHIP: ZADOK

72 Peter Economy, "17 Wise Nelson Mandela Quotes That Will Inspire Your Success," Inc.com, July 21, 2018, https://www.inc.com/peter-economy/17-wise-nelson-mandela-quotes-that-will-inspire-your-success.html.

73 Tom Brokaw, The Greatest Generation (New York: Random House, 1998).

74 "US Population by Age and Generation in 2020," Knoema, April 16, 2020, https://knoema.com/infographics/egyydzc/us-population-by-age-and-generation-in-2020.

75 Michael Dimock, "Defining Generations: Where Millennials End and Generation Z Begins," Pew Research Center, January 17, 2019, https://www.pewresearch.org/fact-tank/2019/01/17/where-millennials-end-and-generation-z-begins/.

76 Dimock, "Defining Generations."

77 Jonah Engel Bromwich, "We Asked Generation Z to Pick a Name. It Wasn't Generation Z," New York Times, January 31, 2018, https://www.nytimes.com/2018/01/31/style/generation-z-name.html.

78 Marty Smith, "Why Is the New Generation Called 'Gen Z?' And Why Did We Start with 'Gen X?'," Willamette Week, April 17, 2018, https://www.

wweek.com/news/2018/04/17/why-is-the-new-generation-called-gen-z-and-why-did-we-start-with-gen-x/.

79 Eccl 1:4

80 "2020 World Population by Country," World Population Review, accessed October 9, 2020, https://worldpopulationreview.com/.

81 "2020 World Population by Country."

82 David Stillman and Jonah Stillman, Gen Z @ Work: How the Next Generation Is Transforming the Workplace (New York: Harper Business, 2017).

83 Stillman and Stillman, 74.

84 World Impact TV, "World Impact—GenZ: Generation of Worship," Vimeo video, 28:29, October 10, 2019, https://vimeo.com/365674532.

85 1 Chr 15:11

86 1 Chr 24:3

87 2 Sm 15:23

88 1 Kgs 1:8, 32

89 1 Chr 29:22

90 Ez 40:46

91 Ez 44:15

92 Ps 24:3–6

93 Jerry Bridges, The Joy of Fearing God (Colorado Springs: WaterBrook Press, 2004), 241.

94 See Lv 10

95 "Worship," Biblical Training, accessed July 2, 2020, https://www.biblical-training.org/library/worship.

96 Lk 22:48

97 Acts 4:36–37

98 Acts 5:1–2

99 Acts 5:3, author's paraphrase.

100 Acts 5:8

101 World Impact TV, "World Impact—GenZ: Generation of Worship," Vimeo video, 28:30, October 10, 2019, https://vimeo.com/365674532.

102 Jn 4:19–24

103 Ps 138:1

104 A. W. Tozer, Tozer for the Christian Leader: A 365-Day Devotional (Chicago: Moody Publishers, 2015), 2.

105 Michael L. Brown, Authentic Fire: A Response to John MacArthur's Strange Fire (Lake Mary, FL: Creation House, 2015), 248.

106 Jonathan Edwards, A Treatise Concerning Religious Affections (New York, 1829), 12, https://books.google.com/books?id=6BtEAQAAMAAJ.

CHAPTER FOUR A GENERATION BORN FOR THE SPIRIT: ZECHARIAH AND ZERUBBABEL

107 Zec 4:6

108 Acts 2:1–4

109 Megan Goodwin, "Reality vs Authenticity," C21Media, May 16, 2017, https://www.c21media.net/perspective/reality-vs-authenticity/.

110 Thomas L. Friedman, The World Is Flat: A Brief History of the Twenty-First Century (New York: Farrar, Straus and Giroux, 2005).

111 Moonjang Lee, "Rethinking the Nature of Christian Mission: A South Korean Perspective," in The State of Missiology Today: Global Innovations in Christian Witness, ed. Charles E. Van Engen (Downers Grove, IL: IVP Academic, 2016), 128.

112 John W. Yelland, "Study: Teens Twice as Likely to Identify as Atheist or LGBT," KUTV, January 24, 2018, https://kutv.com/news/nation-world/study-teens-twice-as-likely-to-identify-as-atheist-or-lgbt.

113 Michael Lipka, "A Closer Look at America's Rapidly Growing Religious 'Nones,'" Pew Research Center, May 13, 2015, https://www.pewresearch.org/fact-tank/2015/05/13/a-closer-look-at-americas-rapidly-growing-religious-nones/.

114 "Atheism Doubles among Generation Z," Barna Group, January 24, 2018, https://www.barna.com/research/atheism-doubles-among-generation-z/.

115 David Kinnaman and Mark Matlock, Faith for Exiles: 5 Ways for a New Generation to Follow Jesus in Digital Babylon (Grand Rapids, MI: Baker Books, 2019), 32, 221–22.

116 James Emery White, Meet Generation Z: Understanding and Reaching the New Post-Christian World (Grand Rapids, MI: Baker Books, 2019) 58, 65–66.

117 "2020 World Population by Country," World Population Review, accessed October 9, 2020, https://worldpopulationreview.com/.

118 Mt 5:6

119 A. H. Sayce, An Introduction to the Books of Ezra, Nehemiah, and Esther (London, UK: Religious Tract Society, 1885), 6.

120 Ezr 5:1–2

121 Zec 4:6–7

122 1 Jn 4:4

123 Zec 4:6

124 Dan Graves, "Article #15: Our Hearts Are Restless," Christian History Institute, accessed July 1, 2020, https://christianhistoryinstitute.org/incontext/article/augustine.

125 G. I. Williamson, The Westminster Shorter Catechism: For Study Classes (Phillipsburg, NJ: P & R Publishers, 2003), 1.

126 Zec 4:6–7

CHAPTER FIVE A GENERATION BORN FOR HOPE: ZEPHANIAH

127 Sally C. Curtin and Melonie Heron, "Death Rates Due to Suicide and Homicide among Persons Aged 10–24: United States, 2000–2017" NHCS Data Brief no. 352 (October 2019): 1, https://www.cdc.gov/nchs/data/databriefs/db352-h.pdf.

128 Martin Luther, The Table Talk of Martin Luther (London: Bell & Daldy,

1876), 146, https://books.google.com/books?id=ZUAuAAAAYAAJ&p-g=PA146&dq.

129 "Hal Lindsey," Goodreads, accessed November 25, 2020, https://www.goodreads.com/author/quotes/11197.Hal_Lindsey.

130 "Major Depression," National Institute of Mental Health, last updated February 2019, https://www.nimh.nih.gov/health/statistics/major-depression.

131 "Depression," World Health Organization, January 30, 2020, https://www.who.int/news-room/fact-sheets/detail/depression.

132 Ellie Polack, "New Cigna Study Reveals Loneliness at Epidemic Levels in America," Cigna, May 1, 2018, https://www.cigna.com/newsroom/news-releases/2018/new-cigna-study-reveals-loneliness-at-epidemic-levels-in-america.

133 Fast Facts card from the Global Youth Culture U.S. Report (Pompano Beach, FL: OneHope, 2020), 18, https://onehope.net/wp-content/uploads/2020/09/GYC-Fast-Facts-Card-Final.pdf.

134 "Suicide Facts," SAVE, accessed June 23, 2020, https://save.org/about-suicide/suicide-facts/.

135 H. Hedegaard, S. C. Curtin, and M. Warner, "Suicide Mortality in the United States, 1999–2017," NCHS Data Brief, no. 330, November 2018 (Hyattsville, MD: National Center for Health Statistics, 2018), https://www.cdc.gov/nchs/products/databriefs/db330.htm.

136 "Suicide," National Institute of Mental Health, last updated September 2020, https://www.nimh.nih.gov/health/statistics/suicide.shtml.

137 Global Youth Culture U.S. Report, 17.

138 Lea Winerman, "By the Numbers: Stress on Campus,"Monitor on Psychology 48, no. 8 (September 2017): 88, https://www.apa.org/monitor/2017/09/numbers.

139 Sophie Bethune, "Gen Z More Likely to Report Mental Health Concerns,"-Monitor on Psychology 50, no. 1 (January 2019): 20, https://www.apa.org/monitor/2019/01/gen-z.

140 "2020 World Population by Country," World Population Review, accessed October 9, 2020, https://worldpopulationreview.com/.

141 Kelly Springs-Kelley, "Here's Why You Shouldn't Confuse Gen Z with Millennials," A Little Bird, January 18, 2019, https://old.alittle-bird.com/heres-why-you-shouldnt-confuse-gen-z-with-millennials/.

142 "2019 Adobe Brand Content Survey," Adobe, February 7, 2019, https://www.slideshare.net/adobe/2019-adobe-brand-content-survey.

143 Jean M. Twenge, "Have Smartphones Destroyed a Generation?," The Atlantic, September 2017, https://www.theatlantic.com/magazine/archive/2017/09/has-the-smartphone-destroyed-a-generation/534198/.

144 Eugenia A. Ives, "iGeneration: The Social Cognitive Effects of Digital Technology on Teenagers" (master's thesis, Dominican University of California, 2012), 39, https://eric.ed.gov/?id=ED543278.

145 Alanna Vagianos, "30 Alarming Statistics That Show the Reality of Sexual Violence in America," HuffPost, April 6, 2017, https://www.huffpost.com/en-

try/sexual-assault-statistics_n_58e24c14e4b0c777f788d24f.

146 "Statistics about Sexual Violence," National Sexual Violence Resource Center, 2015, https://www.nsvrc.org/sites/default/files/publications_nsvrc_factsheet_media-packet_statistics-about-sexual-violence_0.pdf.

147 Catherine Townsend and Alyssa A. Rheingold, Estimating a Child Sexual Abuse Prevalence Rate for Practitioners: A Review of Child Sexual Abuse Prevalence Studies (Charleston, SC: Darkness to Light, 2013), 21, https://www.d2l.org/wp-content/uploads/2017/02/PREVALENCE-RATE-WHITE-PAPER-D2L.pdf.

148 "15–24 Year Olds Account for Half of All New STD Infections," Centers for Disease Control and Prevention, last reviewed January 25, 2021, https://www.cdc.gov/std/life-stages-populations/adolescents-youngadults.htm.

149 US Department of Agriculture, Agricultural Research for a Better Tomorrow: Commemorating the Hatch Act Centennial, 1887–1987 (Washington, DC: US Dept. of Agriculture, 1987), 151.

150 Zep 1:2

151 Zep 1:4

152 Zep 3:14–17

153 Heb 12:7–9

154 See Lv 20:10

155 Jn 8:7, author's paraphrase.

156 Jn 8:10–11

157 Mt 12:20–21; Is 42:3–4

158 Ps 130:7

159 Lam 3:24–25

160 Jas 5:11

161 Jer 29:11

162 Lewis A. Drummond, Spurgeon: Prince of Preachers (Grand Rapids, MI: Kregel Publications, 1992), 238–40.

163 "Spurgeon's Service at Surrey Gardens," Christianity.com, May 3, 2010, https://www.christianity.com/church/church-history/timeline/1801-1900/spurgeons-service-at-surrey-gardens-11630503.html.

164 "11 Reasons Spurgeon Was Depressed," The Spurgeon Center, July 11, 2017, https://www.spurgeon.org/resource-library/blog-entries/11-reasons-spurgeon-was-depressed/.

165 Drummond, Prince of Preachers, 243–245.

166 "The Truth, the Whole Truth and Nothing but the Truth," Lawyers.com, June 19, 2012, https://blogs.lawyers.com/attorney/litigation/the-truth-the-whole-truth-and-nothing-but-the-truth-21450/.

167 "The Truth, the Whole Truth and Nothing but the Truth," Lawyers.com.

168 "Gen Z and Morality: What Teens Believe (So Far)," Barna, October 9, 2018, https://www.barna.com/research/gen-z-morality/.

169 Rv 21:8, emphasis added.

170 Is 5:14 (kjv)

171 Prv 12:22

172 Ty Kiisel, "Without It, No Real Success Is Possible," Forbes, February 5, 2013, https://www.forbes.com/sites/tykiisel/2013/02/05/without-it-no-real-success-is-possible/.

173 "Business Ethics Quotes," Small Businessify.com, accessed July 1, 2020, https://smallbusinessify.com/business-ethics-quotes/.

174 Peter Economy, "21 Zig Ziglar Quotes to Inspire Your Success in Life and Business," Inc., October 2, 2015, https://www.inc.com/peter-economy/21-zig-ziglar-quotes-to-inspire-your-success-in-life-and-business.html.

175 Dan Western, "60 Truly Motivational Joyce Meyer Quotes," WealthyGorilla, accessed July 1, 2020, https://wealthygorilla.com/60-joyce-meyer-quotes/.

176 Richard G. Geldard, The Spiritual Teachings of Ralph Waldo Emerson (Great Barrington, MA: Lindisfarne Books, 2001), 163.

177 Merriam-Webster.com Dictionary, s.v. "Integer," accessed July 1, 2020, https://www.merriam-webster.com/dictionary/integer.

178 Jas 1:8 (kjv)

179 "If You Tell the Truth, You Don't Have to Remember Anything," Quotespedia, accessed July 1, 2020, https://www.quotespedia.org/authors/m/mark-twain/if-you-tell-the-truth-you-dont-have-to-remember-anything-mark-twain/.

180 Is 59:14 (kjv)

181 Merriam-Webster.com Dictionary, s.v. "Gnosis," accessed July 1, 2020, https://www.merriam-webster.com/dictionary/gnosis.

182 William Wilson, "Spirit Empowered Living: Integrity," lecture, Oral Roberts University, Tulsa, OK, October 1, 2019.

183 Jn 14:15

184 1 Jn 1:6; 2:3–4

185 1 Thes 5:23

186 "Quotes on TRUST," LeadershipNow, accessed July 1, 2020, https://www.leadershipnow.com/trustquotes.html.

187 Lk 19:8

188 Lk 19:9–10

189 Ps 41:11–12

CHAPTER SEVEN A GENERATION BORN FOR COMMITMENT: ZIPPORAH

190 Vinson Synan and Billy Wilson, As the Waters Cover the Sea (Tulsa, OK: Empowered Books, 2021), 120.

191 Doug Bock Clark, "The American Missionary and the Uncontacted Tribe," GQ, August 22, 2019, https://www.gq.com/story/john-chau-missionary-and-uncontacted-tribe.

192 Synan and Wilson, As the Waters Cover the Sea, 120.

193 Synan and Wilson, 121–22.

194 John Chau, letter to family, November 17, 2018.

195 William Garden Blaikie, The Personal Life of David Livingstone (Frankfurt

am Main, Germany: Outlook, 2019), 81.

196 "David Livingstone Biography," Biography Online, accessed July 2, 2020, https://www.biographyonline.net/adventurers/david-livingstone.html.

197 "David Livingstone," Faith Bible Baptist Church, accessed July 2, 2020, http://www.fbbc.com/messages/Livingstone.htm.

198 William Garden Blaikie, The Personal Life of David Livingstone (London: J. Murray, 1881), 270.

199 Justin D. Livingstone, "Livingstone's Life & Expeditions," ed. Adrian S. Wisnicki and Megan Ward, 2nd ed., Livingstone Online, University of Maryland Libraries, 2015, https://livingstoneonline.org/life-and-times/living-stone-s-life-expeditions.

200 Patsy Lewis, Simply Praying: 52 Weeks with God (Bloomington, IN: Beacon Hill Press, 2007), 107.

201 George Albert Shepperson, "Influence," Encyclopaedia Britannica, April 27, 2020, https://www.britannica.com/biography/David-Livingstone/Influence.

202 J. Warren Smith, "See How These Christians Love One Another," Christian History no. 105 (2013), https://christianhistoryinstitute.org/magazine/article/see-how-these-christians-love.

203 Acts 1:8

204 "3144. martus," Bible Hub, accessed July 2, 2020, https://biblehub.com/greek/3144.htm.

205 "Bridegroom of blood" refers to circumcision.

206 Ex 4:24–26

207 Acts 16:3

208 Gal 5:2; Acts 16:4

209 Acts 16:1

210 Acts 16:3

211 Rom 2:28–29

212 Col 2:11

213 J. Oswald Sanders, Spiritual Leadership: Principles of Excellence for Every Believer (Chicago: Moody Publishers, 2017), 184.

214 "David Livingstone," Goodreads, accessed October 15, 2020, https://www.goodreads.com/author/quotes/211925.David_Livingstone.

215 Amy Adkins, "Millennials: The Job-Hopping Generation," Gallup, December 16, 2019, https://www.gallup.com/workplace/231587/millennials-job-hopping-generation.aspx.

CHAPTER EIGHT A GENERATION BORN FOR INFLUENCE: ZERUIAH

216 John C. Maxwell, The 21 Irrefutable Laws of Leadership (Nashville: Thomas Nelson, 2008), 13.

217 Eric Spitznagel, "Generation Z Is Bigger than Millennials—and They're Out to Change the World," New York Post, January 25, 2020, https://nypost.com/2020/01/25/generation-z-is-bigger-than-millennials-and-theyre-out-to-change-the-world/.

218 Jeff Fromm, "How Much Financial Influence Does Gen Z Have?" Forbes, January 10, 2018, https://www.forbes.com/sites/jefffromm/2018/01/10/what-you-need-to-know-about-the-financial-impact-of-gen-z-influence.

219 "Gen Z: How Influence Becomes Power," Barclays, accessed July 2, 2020, https://www.investmentbank.barclays.com/our-insights/generation-z/genera-tion-z-how-influence-becomes-power.html.

220 Tracy Francis and Fernanda Hoefel, "'True Gen': Generation Z and Its Implications for Companies," McKinsey & Company, November 12, 2018, https://www.mckinsey.com/industries/consumer-packaged-goods/our-insights/true-gen-generation-z-and-its-implications-for-companies.

221 Michael Pankowski, "Gen Z Will Change the World," PRWeek, October 7, 2019, https://www.prweek.com/article/1661742/gen-z-will-change-world.

222 Kim Parker and Ruth Igielnik, "On the Cusp of Adulthood and Facing an Uncertain Future: What We Know about Gen Z So Far," Pew Research Center, May 14, 2020, https://www.pewsocialtrends.org/essay/on-the-cusp-of-adulthood-and-facing-an-uncertain-future-what-we-know-about-gen-z-so-far.

223 Parker and Igielnik, "What We Know about Gen Z So Far."

224 "Generation Z Statistics," 99Firms, accessed July 2, 2020, https://99firms.com/blog/generation-z-statistics/.

225 Travis Clark and Amanda Perelli, "An 8-Year-Old Boy Is Making $26 Million a Year on YouTube Reviewing Toys," Business Insider, December 18, 2019, https://www.businessinsider.com/ryans-world-boy-makes-26-million-per-year-on-youtube-2019-12.

226 Otis and Frank Cary, "How Old Were Christ's Disciples?" The Biblical World 50, no. 1 (July 1917): 3–12.

227 Roy Jenkins, "The Welsh Revival," BBC, last updated June 16, 2009, https://www.bbc.co.uk/religion/religions/christianity/history/welshrevival_1.shtml.

228 Robert I. Bradshaw, "Bending the Church to Save the World: The Welsh Revival of 1904," Theological Studies, January 1, 1995, https://theologicals-tudies.org.uk/article_welshrevival.html.

229 Brandon Showalter, "Great Awakening on Global Scale Is Near, Reminiscent of Welsh Revival, Wallace Henley Predicts," Christian Examiner, May 6, 2019, https://www.christianexaminer.com/article/great-awakening-on-global-scale-is-near-reminiscent-of-welsh-revival-wallace-henley-predicts/52770.htm.

230 Earle E. Cairns, An Endless Line of Splendor: Revivals and Their Leaders from the Great Awakening to the Present (Eugene, OR: Wipf & Stock, 2015), 195–96.

231 Ed Hird and Janice Hird, "Evan Roberts in the Land of Revivals," Ed Hird's Blog, June 1, 2019, https://edhird.com/2019/06/01/evan-roberts-in-the-land-of-revivals/.

232 Wallace Henley, Call Down Lightning: What the Welsh Revival of 1904 Reveals about the End Times (Nashville: Emanate Books, 2019), 75.

233 Stephen B. Oates, Let the Trumpet Sound: A Life of Martin Luther King, Jr. (New York: HarperCollins, 1994), 5.

234 "Dr. Martin Luther King Education," Dr. Martin Luther King (website),

accessed July 2, 2020, http://drmartinlutherking.net/martin-luther-king-education.

235 Linda K. Fuller, ed., National Days/National Ways: Historical, Political, and Religious Celebrations around the World (Westport, CT: Greenwood Publishing, 2004), 314.

236 Sabrina Crewe and Frank Walsh, The Montgomery Bus Boycott (Milwaukee, WI: Gareth Stevens, 2003), 17–18.

237 Manning Marable and Leith Mullings, eds., Let Nobody Turn Us Around: Voices on Resistance, Reform, and Renewal: An African American Anthology (Lanham, MA: Rowman & Littlefield, 1999), 391–92.

238 L. Mpho Mahunda, ed., African American Almanac, 7th ed, (Farmington Hills, MI: Gale, 1997), quoted in "The Life of Martin Luther King, Jr.," The Seattle Times, 2017, accessed July 2, 2020, http://special.seattletimes.com/o/special/mlk/king/biography.html.

239 "The Life of Martin Luther King, Jr," The Seattle Times.

240 "Martin Luther King Wins the Nobel Prize for Peace," New York Times, October 15, 1964, https://archive.nytimes.com/www.nytimes.com/learning/general/onthisday/big/1014.html.

241 History.com Editors, "Civil Rights Act of 1964," History Channel, last updated January 25, 2021, https://www.history.com/topics/black-history/civil-rights-act.

242 History.com Editors, "Voting Rights Act of 1965," History Channel, last updated January 26, 2021, https://www.history.com/topics/black-history/voting-rights-act.

243 Nikita Stewart, "'I've Been to the Mountaintop,' Dr. King's Last Sermon Annotated," New York Times, April 2, 2018, https://www.nytimes.com/interactive/2018/04/02/us/king-mlk-last-sermon-annotated.html.

244 History.com Editors, "Martin Luther King, Jr., Assassination," History Channel, last updated April 1, 2021, https://www.history.com/topics/black-history/martin-luther-king-jr-assassination.

245 Hannah Hutyra, "123 of the Most Powerful Martin Luther King Quotes Ever," KeepInspiring.me, accessed July 2, 2020, from https://www.keepinspiring.me/martin-luther-king-jr-quotes/.

246 Dominic-Madori Davis, "The Action Generation: How Gen Z Really Feels about Race, Equality, and Its Role in the Historic George Floyd Protests, Based on a Survey of 39,000 Young Americans," Business Insider, June 10, 2020, https://www.businessinsider.com/how-gen-z-feels-about-george-floyd-protests-2020-6.

247 Ps 127:4

248 2 Sm 2